Orkney and Scapa Flow at War 1939–45

Orkney and Scapa Flow at War 1939–45

Craig Armstrong

First published in Great Britain in 2020 by
Pen & Sword Military
An imprint of
Pen & Sword Books Ltd
Yorkshire – Philadelphia

Copyright © Craig Armstrong, 2020

ISBN 978 1 47389 9 209

The right of Craig Armstrong to be identified as Author of this work has been asserted by him in accordance with the Copyright, Designs and Patents Act 1988.

A CIP catalogue record for this book is
available from the British Library.

All rights reserved. No part of this book may be reproduced or transmitted in any form or by any means, electronic or mechanical including photocopying, recording or by any information storage and retrieval system, without permission from the Publisher in writing.

Printed and bound in England by CPI Group (UK) Ltd, Croydon, CR0 4YY

Pen & Sword Books Limited incorporates the imprints of Atlas, Archaeology, Aviation, Discovery, Family History, Fiction, History, Maritime, Military, Military Classics, Politics, Select, Transport, True Crime, Air World, Frontline Publishing, Leo Cooper, Remember When, Seaforth Publishing, The Praetorian Press, Wharncliffe Local History, Wharncliffe Transport, Wharncliffe True Crime and White Owl.

For a complete list of Pen & Sword titles please contact

PEN & SWORD BOOKS LIMITED
47 Church Street, Barnsley, South Yorkshire, S70 2AS, England
E-mail: enquiries@pen-and-sword.co.uk
Website: www.pen-and-sword.co.uk

Or

PEN AND SWORD BOOKS
1950 Lawrence Rd, Havertown, PA 19083, USA
E-mail: Uspen-and-sword@casematepublishers.com
Website: www.penandswordbooks.com

For My Parents

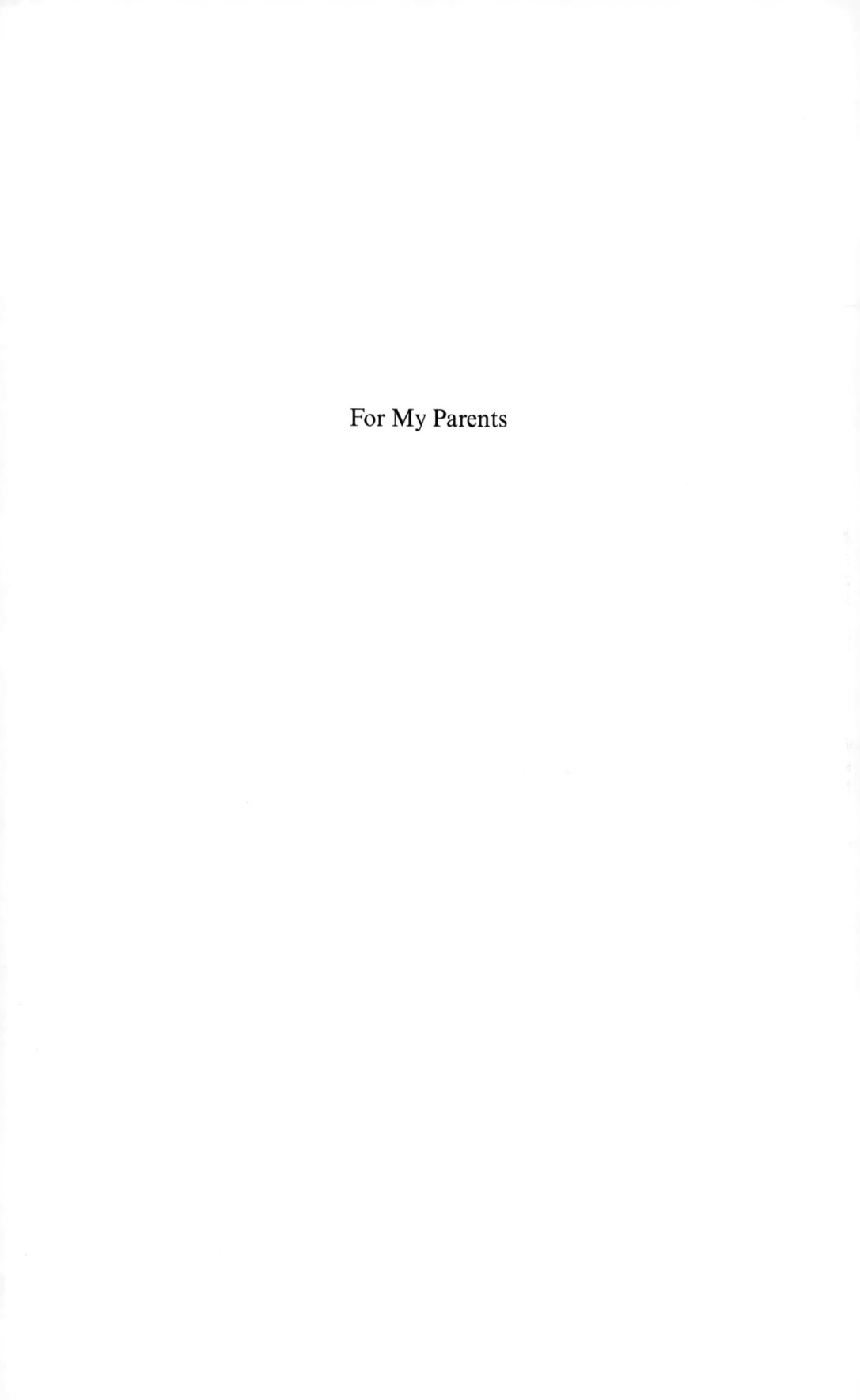

Contents

Introduction   viii

Chapter 1   1939: The Gathering Storm   1
Chapter 2   1940: The Bleakest Year   13
Chapter 3   1941: A Losing Battle   52
Chapter 4   1942: Struggling on   73
Chapter 5   1943: Turning the Tide   95
Chapter 6   1944: D-Day and Beyond   116
Chapter 7   1945: Peace at Last   124

Endnotes   129
Index   134

Introduction

An archipelago lying some 10 miles off the north coast of Scotland, Orkney consists of no fewer than sixty-seven separate islands, twenty of which are inhabited. The largest island is known as the Mainland and it hosts the administrative centre of the islands, Kirkwall. Orkney has a very storied history with habitation dating back to at least the Mesolithic era while the origin of the name itself is pre-Roman in origin.

The earliest dated settlement, Knap of Howar on Papa Westray, dates to the Neolithic period. The farmstead there is believed to be the oldest preserved standing building in northern Europe. There are many ancient sites which tourists can visit on the islands. The settlement of Skara Brae, at Bay of Skaill, on the west coast of the Mainland, is the best-preserved example of a Neolithic settlement in Europe, dating back to approximately 3,100 BC. The settlement is older than either Stonehenge or the Pyramids and is sometimes referred to as Scotland's Pompeii, the site has gained UNESCO World Heritage Site status. There are several similar sites which have been explored to a greater or lesser extent. They include the farmstead at Knap of Howar, mentioned above, a settlement at Rinyo on Rousay and another at Links of Noltland on Westray. Other ancient sites include numerous standing stones, such as the Ring of Brodgar and the Standing Stones of Stenness, as well as the Maeshowe passage grave, on the Mainland.

There are also extensive Iron Age remains on the islands with roundhouses and the impressive round stone brochs. One of the most impressive of these broch sites is Burroughstone Broch on the north-east coast of Shapinsay, overlooking the North Sea.

INTRODUCTION ix

Skara Brae. (GNU, CC 3.0, John Burka)

Entrance to Maeshowe passage grave. (Public Domain)

Burroughston Broch. (Bob Jones / Burroughston Broch, Shapinsay / CC BY-SA 2.0)

By the latter part of the Iron Age, when many of the brochs were built, the islands had become the property of the Picts.

In 875 AD the islands were annexed by the Norwegian King and this occupation has left the islands with a distinctive Norse-influenced culture. It is not known when the Norse inhabitants converted to Christianity but there is an apocryphal story that it came forcibly at the hands of King Olaf Tryggvasson in 995 AD. One of the most famous of the Norse inhabitants was Thorfinn the Mighty who ruled Orkney alongside his brothers and who eventually extended his empire across the sea from Dublin to Shetland. Thorfinn's successors were plagued by internal feuds within the ruling family and these internecine squabbles culminated in the martyring of Magnus Erlendsson at the hands of his cousin. This resulted in the construction of St Magnus' Cathedral. There are many sites at which reminders of the islands' Norse heritage can be seen, including the tidal island settlements at Brough of Birsay. It was not until 1468 that Orkney was formally absorbed by Scotland and the islands therefore possess a unique and vibrant culture.

St Magnus Cathedral. (CC 3.0)

During the First World War Scapa Flow was the home base of the Royal Navy's Home Fleet and it was from here that the Home Fleet left for the Battle of Jutland in 1916. On 5 June 1916 HMS *Hampshire* (which had recently taken part in the Battle of Jutland) was ordered to set sail for Russia carrying the Secretary of State for War, Lord Kitchener, on a diplomatic mission. Shortly after her departure in poor weather off Marwick Head, Orkney, the ship hit a German mine and sank with the loss of 737 lives, including Lord Kitchener. There were only 12 survivors.

On 12 January 1918 there was another naval disaster at Orkney. Two destroyers, HMS *Narborough* and HMS *Opal* were patrolling to the east of the islands when they were ordered to return due to bad weather. Unfortunately, the two ships were caught in a blizzard and with zero visibility the ships came to grief on the rocks at Hesta off the coast of South Ronaldsay. Both ships were utterly wrecked and from the two crews there was only one survivor, Able Seaman William Sissons.

At the end of the war the German High Fleet was brought to Scapa Flow where the Germans managed to scuttle many of the ships. Their remains have provided a rich environment for history-minded diving enthusiasts. The Scapa Flow Visitor Centre at Lyness on Hoy provides visitors with a vibrant and interesting account of the islands during the two World Wars.

Kitchener Memorial at Marwick Head. (Irene Moore)

INTRODUCTION xiii

Kitchener plaque. (Irene Moore)

Wartime relics, including a naval gun. (Irene Moore)

Wartime remains abound on Orkney. (Irene Moore)

CHAPTER 1

1939: The Gathering Storm

The Admiralty was well aware of the threat posed by submarine warfare; after all, Britain had nearly been knocked out of the First World War by unrestricted submarine warfare. Convoy systems were already in place for many, but not all, merchant vessels but the military responses to the threat of the U-boat menace were rather more problematic. In the first month of the war the Admiralty used fast aircraft carriers escorted by destroyers, organized into hunter-killer groups, to patrol likely areas, but this was to prove disastrous and provided Orkney with its first fatalities of the war.

On 14 September the aircraft carrier HMS *Ark Royal* was unsuccessfully attacked by a U-boat but lessons were not immediately learned and just three days later the converted aircraft carrier HMS *Courageous* was leading its own hunter-killer group in the Western Approaches.[1] During the evening of 17 September, while patrolling off the coast of Ireland, she was called to the assistance of a British merchant vessel which had been attacked. All of the ship's aircraft had landed and a fresh wave was preparing to launch when she was struck by two torpedoes fired from *U-29*. Electrical power immediately failed and the carrier capsized and sank within twenty minutes of being struck; 519 of her crew were lost.

Amongst the casualties was Stoker 1st Class John Liddle Delday (43), a native of Stromness. A widower, he was the son of William and Margaret Shearer Delday who lived at Westquoys

2 ORKNEY AND SCAPA FLOW AT WAR 1939–45

HMS Courageous. *(Public Domain)*

HMS Courageous *sinking. (Public Domain)*

Farm, Twatt, Birsay. Stoker Delday was a naval veteran having served for 22 years and was living with his parents, working as an electrical engineer, at the time of his call-up. Another local casualty was Stoker 1st Class George Robertson (32) who had married a Kirkwall woman. He left a widow, Grace Kirkness Robertson, and his parents, James and Catherine Robertson. Grace Robertson, widely known by her maiden name of Maxwell, was staying with her parents in Kirkwall, along with her 5-year-old daughter, at the time of her husband's death. Three days after the loss of the *Courageous* Mrs Robertson told the *Orkney Herald* that she had still received no news of her husband. Stoker Delday's sister, Florence, who worked at Messrs James Flett & Sons, Kirkwall, also said that the family had received no news. By 27 September Mrs Robertson had been informed that her husband had lost his life. She was described as being grief-stricken but moved by the many messages of condolence which had been sent to her. The family of Stoker Delday, however, still had news that he was only being declared as missing, but must surely have feared the worst by this stage. The two men were close friends and both are commemorated on the Plymouth Naval Memorial.

October opened with sad news for the residents of Burray when it was announced that a local man who was serving with the Royal Naval Reserve (RNR) had lost his life in an accidental drowning. Seaman John R. Sutherland had been born at Milhouse and spent his boyhood and youth on Burray, where he was extremely popular. It was believed that Seaman Sutherland had drowned on the south coast of England where he had been due to join his ship.[2]

The only battle-worthy ship left at Scapa in the early hours of 14 October was HMS *Royal Oak*, a First World War era battleship whose crew-list included a large number of boys under the age of 18. The only other large vessel present that night was the ageing seaplane carrier HMS *Pegasus*, which was anchored several miles away and invisible in the darkness of the early hours. Shortly after 1am a small explosion was heard by some of the crew of the *Royal Oak* and the anchor chain ran out. Most believed that an explosion of some sort had occurred in the forward inflammable store and, other than a check on magazine temperatures, most of those who had been awakened returned to their quarters. Skipper John Gatt of the drifter *Daisy II*, which had been lying alongside the battleship, heard the explosion and conferred with the officer of the watch aboard the *Royal Oak*. Noticing that there were straw and wooden staves floating on the water alongside and knowing that this was usually used as packing for ships' stores, and that stores had been brought aboard *Royal Oak* the day before, he assumed that a minor internal explosion had occurred.

Approximately ten minutes later there were three larger explosions which caused a loss of electric power as well as destroying the boys', stokers' and marines' messes; then an unexplained fireball swept through part of the ship from a secondary explosion. The ageing battleship quickly listed to starboard and water flooded through open portholes causing a far more serious list to develop. Less than ten minutes after the second set of explosions the battleship sank. Some men were able to scramble into a boat, others managed to clamber aboard the drifter *Daisy II* which had been lying alongside *Royal Oak*, while others found themselves in the water. The majority, however, remained trapped aboard the battleship as she went down.

For those in the water this was the beginning of a nightmare which took many more lives. The night was very dark, no lights were showing and the surface of the icy water was quickly covered in oil. Some, choking and gasping, struggled to the rocky shoreline nearby only to succumb to exposure or to be killed as they attempted to scale the cliffs in darkness.

The accepted explanation of the loss of the *Royal Oak* was that a German special operation undertaken by *U-47* under the command of Kapitänleutnant Günther Prien had sneaked through the defences of Scapa Flow, hit the battleship with one torpedo of its first volley and had then returned and hit the battleship with another volley of three torpedoes. Certainly, that was the version which was quickly relayed in German propaganda broadcasts which made Prien into an instant national hero. The Admiralty also confirmed this version of events, but recent research has revealed a number of doubts over the claim that Prien and *U-47* had made the successful attack. Certainly, Prien's log contains huge errors which make his account of events very suspect and he later made claims which were proven false, including that he had sunk the cruiser HMS *Norfolk*. Prien also claimed that he had fired at and damaged two battleships on the night of the *Royal Oak* sinking. This was of course impossible as the only other major ship present was the *Pegasus* and, from where Prien would have fired at the *Royal Oak*, it would have been impossible to see the other ship.

Doubt was also cast on the official version of events by survivors and by other German submarine crewmen.[3] Some have made, largely unsubstantiated, claims that sabotage may have caused the loss of the ship but the most likely cause is still a torpedo attack (whether made by Prien or an unnamed commander).

Whatever the causes of the explosions which sank the *Royal Oak*, the crew who survived faced terrible conditions as the battleship went down. No-one had heard the explosions outside the battleship and the drifter and for some time the survivors of the sinking were largely on their own in the cold, dark, waters of the Flow. One of these survivors was local man Herbert Johnston from St Mary's. Johnston was one of the few stokers to escape. Having heard the first explosion he had grown uneasy and went to check on a refrigeration machine for which he was responsible. At this point he heard the other explosions and made for the deck. He managed to climb onto the picket boat but as more men tried to climb aboard this overturned and he was thrown into the water. After swimming for some time, he was picked up by the *Daisy II*.

While the HMS *Royal Oak* was sinking and many of her crew were perishing in the cold waters of the Flow, the majority of the people of Orkney slept on completely unaware of the disaster which was unfolding in their midst. There were few people around and little to see as the once-mighty battleship blazed internally as it sank; no lights were immediately visible. On the streets of Kirkwall, PC David H. Allan, who had friends amongst the crew of the battleship, did not notice anything amiss and believed that this was just another ordinary night. He was unaware that at least one of his friends was, at that moment, swimming for his life just a few miles away. Three exhausted survivors managed to swim to shore and walk to Scapa Pier where they roused the sleeping Pier Master. He then telephoned the HMS *Iron Duke* and the commanding officer signalled HMS *Pegasus* (the only other warship near *Royal Oak*) only to be informed by signal that 'Regret *Royal Oak* has been sunk'.[4]

In the early hours, PC Allan called in at Kirkwall Police Station and while he was there the phone rang and his superiors instructed PC Allan and another constable to go and wake a local bus hirer and take a bus down to Scapa Pier immediately. While they were on their way they encountered a civilian who informed them that the *Royal Oak* had been sunk.

At Lyness, the master of the water-boat *Fountain* was roused by a naval officer who told them to raise steam and set off as the *Royal Oak* had been sunk at her mooring. As the *Fountain* made its way it called at various drifters and alerted them to the catastrophe.

Back at Scapa Pier the fishing drifters were making steam and commencing rescue efforts, in concert with a drifter from *Pegasus*, which were concentrated on the rocky shore and cliffs opposite the stricken battleship. Around 6am the first of the fifteen survivors of the disaster to be landed at Scapa Pier appeared where PC Allan and a small crowd, including the commandeered bus, awaited them. The exhausted and, in many cases, injured survivors were placed on stretchers and transported in the bus to the Kirkwall Hotel, which the Royal Navy had commandeered. Upon arrival at the hotel the less seriously injured were placed in front of a roaring fire, plied with whatever drink they wanted, and interrogated as to their own names, whether they were aware of any other survivors and to what had happened.

PC Allan and his colleague took other survivors to the Fleet Air Arm aerodrome at Hatston where they were quickly made comfortable in spare officers' quarters. One of the men, Stoker Cleverly, later remarked that he did not ordinarily have much time for officers but that those of the Fleet Air Arm had really gone out of their way to take care of them, even providing them with a radio and their own pyjamas.

Three other survivors, who had collapsed unconscious after reaching the shore, were later rescued by a fishing drifter. Taken down to the stokehold the three men, exhausted, frozen and covered in oil, were warmed and the man who was stoking the furnace gave them each a large mug of tea laced with spirits. The three men told the crew that they had earlier heard a man fall as he tried to scale the cliffs, but a search revealed nothing and the drifter took the men to the *Pegasus*.

Some of the fortunate survivors who had managed to struggle aboard one of the few rafts were rescued by drifters and taken to the *Pegasus*. Amongst them were several who were badly burned. Not all of those who had survived exhibited selflessness. One of the burn victims remembered being picked up by a drifter and covered with a blanket. One of the other survivors tried to take the blanket off him only to be told by another that if he tried to touch the unfortunate man again the rest would throw him overboard.

The *Fountain* and the other vessels which it had alerted took three hours to arrive on the scene and were surprised upon arrival that there was seemingly little activity and no lights searching the waters. At around this time the commanding officer of the *Iron Duke* demanded to know why the *Pegasus* had not turned on its searchlight only to be told that he, the commander of the *Pegasus*, did not wish to be torpedoed as well. At this time, of course, there was utter confusion over what had actually happened to the *Royal Oak*.

At least three men from Orkney were aboard the *Royal Oak* with two losing their lives. Bertie Johnston was the son of

Sergeant Johnston and the late Mrs Johnston of St Mary's, Holm and was one of the fortunate uninjured survivors of the disaster. Stoker 2nd Class James William Moar was not so fortunate. The 19-year-old's parents, Alfred Alex and Mary W. Moar, were informed at their home at Westside, Birsay, that their son was not amongst the survivors. The other Orcadian to lose his life was one of the many boys aboard the *Royal Oak*, Boy 1st Class William Gemmell Mitchell Baker. His home was at Well Park, Stromness and it was here that his parents, Robert J. and Mary Elizabeth Baker, were informed of his loss.

A number of those who had survived the initial sinking and managed to swim to the shore seem to have died of exposure during the night as bodies were recovered for several days from the rocky shoreline. PC Allan was himself called down to one such unfortunate a few days after the sinking and found the casualty naked, covered in oil and sprawled on the jagged rocks.

When the true extent of the disaster was known, it was found that 834 of the ship's complement of 1,234 men and boys had been killed or subsequently died of their injuries. A Board of Enquiry recorded that Captain W.G. Benn and his officers had done all that was possible to save their ship.

There had been an eerie foreshadowing of the fate of the *Royal Oak* when in 1936 the battleship had been used in the film 'The Navy Eternal'. In the film the *Royal Oak* had played the role of a rebel battleship which was attacked and sunk by the Royal Navy. The other vessel to star in the film was the anti-aircraft cruiser HMS *Curacoa* which was featured as a British cruiser. Appearing in the film seems to have been a bad omen as the *Curacoa* was also lost during the war, following a collision with the RMS *Queen Mary* in October 1942.

The Orkney Toc-H continued to attract official attention and in October Queen Mary bestowed a gift of £10 to the club while Her Majesty Queen Elizabeth, in her capacity as the patroness of the League of Women Helpers of Toc-H, sent a signed photograph of herself which was prominently displayed over the fireplace in the main clubroom.

HMS Royal Oak *heels over during filming.* (Illustrated London News)

Due to the nature of the military installations on Orkney and the importance of the islands to the war effort, the government was keen to ensure that suitable measures of protection were in place. The Secretary of State for War declared that from 1 December the counties of Orkney and Shetland would be classed as protected areas. Following this date no one other than existing residents, servicemen or police would be permitted to remain in the area or enter it without a permit. Those who were claiming exemption from the order had to provide proof that they were indeed exempt and residents had to produce their national registration identity cards which had to be stamped by a police officer from one of the local forces.

A matter of huge concern to many Orcadians was the propensity of the Luftwaffe to mount attacks on defenceless

Sailors abandon HMS Royal Oak *during filming.* (Illustrated London News)

HMS Royal Oak *at anchor.* (Public Domain)

civilian fishing boats and trawlers. With a large number of Orcadians working in the fishing industry it was feared that this tactic would result in severe casualties for the communities of the islands; sadly, this was proven to be true. On Sunday, 17 December the Leith-based steam trawler *Compagnus* was fishing some 150 miles north-east of May Island in company with the trawler *Colleague* when they were attacked by two German Heinkel He 111 bombers. With her trawl out at the time, the vessel was unable to manoeuvre when the two bombers made their attack. Four bombs were dropped, aimed at the *Compagnus*, but all missed although they did cause some damage. The bombers then circled back to strafe the trawler and 53-year-old deckhand James Swanney courageously dashed onto the deck in an attempt to cut away the trawl, but was killed by machine-gun fire which struck him in the back. The two bombers continued to strafe the trawlers for the next half an hour. The Chief Engineer later said that he thought Mr Swanney was running for cover. Following this initial attack the two trawlers continued fishing, but two hours later they were attacked once more when a total of ten bombs were dropped. Two of these struck the *Compagnus* and caused the ship to sink with the surviving crew, two of whom were injured, being taken aboard the other trawler.

Mr Swanney was a native of Kirkwall but for a number of years had lived at Leith. He had a brother who still lived near Kirkwall and many of the older people in the town remembered him fondly. Local newspapers described his killing as 'a typical example of the cowardly tactics of the Huns'.[5] His body was not recovered and he is commemorated on the Tower Hill Memorial. The account of his attempt to cut away the fishing gear was confirmed and he was later commended for his bravery in May 1940.[6]

The first wartime Christmas saw many efforts made to raise funds for the various wartime charities with dances and other entertainments being commonplace across the islands. On Westray, for example, a dance held at the Pierowall Public

School on 29 December raised the sum of £3 1s 6d, which was donated to the Red Cross Society. The dance had been organized by the WVS and, along with the money raised from the dance, several gifts of spun wool had also been received and the ladies of the WVS were already using the wool to knit comforts for the forces.

CHAPTER 2

1940: The Bleakest Year

The people of Orkney had been speculating on what the first wartime Hogmanay would bring, with many claiming that they thought the majority of folk would remain quietly at home. This view was confounded as large numbers of people – approximately 1,000 – began to gather in Broad Street and on the Market Green shortly before midnight. This was only a little short of what was frequently seen during peacetime, but the celebrations were somewhat more muted as there were, of course, no fireworks and the blackout also had an impact. Ordinarily, Broad Street would have been almost floodlit, but the blackout meant that people struggled to recognise friends and family and the attempts at community singing were somewhat low key.

Just as it seemed that it might indeed be the quietest Hogmanay on record, the sound of the pipes was heard. The pipers were from a Scottish regiment based on Orkney and they were met with loud cheers as they marched up the street before assembling on the green and playing in the New Year. The New Year itself was welcomed in the traditional fashion with songs, hand-shaking and good wishes expressed, along with the significant addition of people wishing each other a 'peaceful New Year'. After this people departed in small groups to embark on the traditional tour of first footing. Observers noted that this activity seemed to have remained as popular as it had ever been during peacetime.[7]

With opportunities for entertainment hard to come by in wartime Orkney, the tours of Ensa entertainers were a welcome break. Throughout the festive period a group known as the 'Tartan Tonics' were touring the islands with their performances open not only to members of the military, but also to the civilian population. The local press heaped praise upon the performers saying that Orcadians could certainly not complain over the quality of the Ensa members who had been sent to the islands. The show was a mixture of music and comedy and featured the radio comedian Willie Lindsay; a comedy double act, Jack Fraser and Miss Ellis Drake; a soprano, Miss Vivien Welsh; and an acrobatic dancer, Miss Dorothy Babette. The producer of the show, Lex McLean, was no stranger to Orkney having played in both Kirkwall and Stromness with 'The Meltonians' concert party before the war. He was well known in sporting circles in both places as he had also turned out for Kirkwall Rovers and Stromness Athletic during his visits.

One of the attractions on offer on New Year's Day was a football match at Bignold Park between Kirkwall City and a Fleet Air Arm side. The game was well attended and spectators were treated to an exciting and hard fought match with the Fleet Air Arm side proving to be amongst the most capable of the service teams in the county. Kirkwall City were without three of their top players due to injury and started the match with only ten men. Despite this handicap, and a frosty pitch, City held their own before their eleventh player took the field and they began to gain the upper hand. After 25 minutes City took the lead only to be immediately pegged back by the airmen. The second half opened with the airmen on top but half-way through the half City once more went ahead only for the airmen to again equalise almost immediately. The final minutes of the contest saw end to end action without further scoring and the match finished in a 2-2 draw.

The first week of the New Year saw a happy event take place at Kirkwall when a local man, who was a soldier with the British Expeditionary Force (BEF) in France, married his sweetheart while home on leave. Private Thomas Rosie, of 8 High Street, Kirkwall, was the bridegroom and the bride was Miss Edna Reid of The Bungalow, Stronsay. With silk unavailable, wartime brides made the most of the clothing that could be obtained and Miss Reid wore a navy-blue coat and hat with matching accessories, while the bridesmaid, Private Rosie's sister, Edna, also wore navy-blue with a grey hat. The best man, Mr Edwin Peace, was a close friend of Private Rosie. Following the ceremony, the bridal party adjourned to the home of Miss Reid's sister, Mrs D. Flett, at Laing Street where a reception was held. The bride was well known as she had worked as an assistant at the Pomona Café before her marriage.

This happy event was followed days later by the sad news that another Orcadian had lost his life while on service and yet again it was the tight-knit community of Burray which was affected. Seaman Norman Duncan Bruce (23) of Gowanbraes, Burray, like many an Orcadian, was a member of the RNR having joined aged 20 and had immediately been called up at the outbreak of war. Trawlers were often assigned to minesweeping work but the Admiralty-owned HMT *Kingston Cornelian* had instead been converted into an anti-submarine warfare trawler and by late 1939 was assigned to the Mediterranean theatre. On the night of 5 January the trawler was operating off Gibraltar when she was involved in a collision with a French merchant vessel, the *Chella*. The collision set off the depth charges which the trawler was carrying and the catastrophic explosion resulted in her sinking very quickly with the loss of all seventeen of her crew, including Seaman Bruce.[8]

Food rationing began on 8 January and even many items which were not placed on the rationed list had their prices fixed by the government. The first food items to be rationed included staples such as sugar, bacon, ham and butter. In an effort to appease people the local press ran articles throughout January which offered reassurance that the rationed goods would be available and that the amounts were generous and fair, along with guides and advice as to how to eke out the portions and to provide nourishment using items which were not yet on the ration.

On 24 January the *Orkney Herald* ran one such article under the headline 'Mainly for Women'. This offered the reassurance that the sugar ration in particular was generous at a weekly ration of ¾lb per person compared to just ½lb during the First World War. Sugar was also available in cafes and teashops without the need for expending ration coupons, while Orcadians were informed that there were large supplies of sugar in dried fruit such as raisins and sultanas available. Housewives were also informed that they should consider using honey and golden syrup as energy foods. As much of the sugar supply was used for cooking, housewives were told that saccharin could be used to replace sugar in tea and coffee and that the sugar substitute was readily available from chemists for 1s per 100 tablets. For those who wished to make their own marmalade or jam additional sugar could be obtained but only with a permit from the local Food Controller and proof that sufficient quantities of fruit had been purchased for the purpose.

The early responses of Orcadians to the imposition of rationing was relatively positive. The *Orkney Herald* enquired of attitudes towards the rationing system of shoppers in the days immediately following the beginning of rationing. The newspaper reported that people were 'quite good-humoured about it' although the butter ration was causing some consternation with one woman ruefully informing the reporter that her boy spread 'nearly a quarter o' a pund every time he spreads a piece'.[9] Local shopkeepers, however, reported slow trade in rationed items and the general impression was that most people had laid in a goodly supply before rationing came into force.

Housewives were also warned to prepare themselves to cope with the meat rationing which was to be introduced in March as it was thought that the official control of the availability of many meat products would have the effect of pushing up prices. The meat ration was to be determined by value and housewives were advised to consider cheaper and less popular cuts. The authorities on Orkney believed that the average ration would amount to approximately 2lbs per head, per week, but this could not be guaranteed. Tripe, oxtail, liver and other offal was not to be rationed and neither were sausages or meat pies containing less than 50 per cent meat, but this would result in vastly increased demand for these items and shortages were possible as a result. Housewives were reassured, however, that government control of prices would mean that the cost of purchasing off-ration meat products would not rise beyond their means. There was no denying, however, that the rationing of meat would result in significant changes to diet and eating habits. The traditional Sunday roast would become a rarity, replaced by stews, and the majority of families would be required to eke out their meat ration for as long as possible. Advice on how to do this was to be offered to housewives (and others) through official pamphlets giving guidance on reduced waste wartime cooking. The Women's Institute and similar bodies would be the heralds for this campaign with pamphlets, lectures and courses available.

It was clear that, as in the last war, the conflict would result in shortages of many items of food and with Orkney's island status it could prove even more difficult for the islanders to obtain some foodstuffs. The Orcadians, however, were a resolute and determined people who had become accustomed to living off their own means and many already had vegetable gardens while others kept their own hens or pigs and there were many crofters on the islands. One dietary staple of the islands was, of course, fish and it was believed that this supply would be maintained despite the greater risks facing fishermen during wartime.

One of the more dangerous careers during the war was to serve aboard the vessels of the Orkney Direct Line. This vital service was maintained throughout the war as a lifeline for the people of the islands and the crews demonstrated great courage in maintaining the service despite the increased risks of wartime sailing. At approximately 9am on 3 February the steamer AS *Rota* was off Orkney when her crew observed an aircraft approaching.

The crew did not react, believing that it was a British machine but, as it drew nearer, they realised it was German. The bomber made six attacks in total, dropping five bombs. Skipper William McIntosh had got his crew under cover but he remained in the wheelhouse steering a zig-zag course which successfully evaded the first four bombs. The final bomb, which dropped close alongside, failed to explode. The crew said that it was only through the skilful steering and calm-headedness of their skipper that they emerged unscathed. The skipper of the *Rota* was from Buckie (but was very well known on Orkney) and her crew included at least one Orcadian, Able Seaman James Tulloch from Eday.[10]

For Orcadians struggling to eke out supplies the newspapers ran regular recipe advice columns with the *Orkney Herald* running a column entitled 'War-Time Recipes'. On 14 February the column featured two recipes. The first was for sausage pudding and this involved only three ingredients, sausage meat, gravy and suet. The second recipe, highlighting the availability and widespread use of fish, was for a simple potato and fish pie.

It would appear that the widely anticipated food shortages also resulted in an upsurge in poaching as the local press contained a raft of notices issued by local factors and various landowners informing Orcadians that anyone found on the land with a gun or dog without express permission would be prosecuted. These included local factor, Henry W. Scarth of Skaill House who gave notice that anyone found with dog or gun on the lands of West Hills, Stromness, or any other part of the estate would be prosecuted and that the gamekeeper had been ordered to report all such trespassers.

Similar warnings were issued for many estates including Woodwick Estate, Evie, Codomo and Stenness. It was not only the poaching of game-birds that was occurring, many seemed to have been in pursuit of rabbits with another factor, Thomas Peace Low of Kirkwall, warning that prosecutions would be taken out against anyone who entered the lands of Hobbister, Orphir, Lesliedale, Highland Park, Mayfield, Hillhead, Crantit,

St Ola and the lands of Trumland, Rousay. This applied not only to trespassers with guns or dogs but also those who damaged 'dykes in pursuit of rabbits'.[11] Meanwhile, Mr Duncan J. Robertson, the factor for the Melsetter Estate, wrote from Kirkwall warning that, as damage had been done to game by people taking dogs over the hills in Hoy and Walls, in the future anyone with a dog which was not on a leash in those areas would henceforth be prosecuted.

Not only was the poaching of game concerning local landowners, warnings were also given regarding the prosecution of people who cut peats or divots from the lands in Holm and St Andrew which belonged to Mr Sutherland Graeme or who removed gravel or sand from the foreshores of St Mary's Bay or Ayre, Holm.

It was not just food which was in short supply. Cloth was also to be rationed and this resulted in a campaign to make-do-and-mend alongside thrifty advice, aimed solely at women, on how to make one's own dresses. Most of the larger stores offered a service whereby they would cut out any simple pattern provided that the material and pattern had been purchased in that store. Housewives were also advised to make their own garments using simple patterns which were frequently featured in the local press.

Many people were going into the shops to obtain coat and suit-length supplies of material for use in the spring, aware that prices would increase in the immediate future. Woollens were especially popular on the isles and shoppers were advised to make the most of sale prices as it was expected that the price of such items would rise considerably.

The rural economy of Orkney continued throughout the war although the farmers and crofters of Orkney faced additional difficulties in getting their produce to market on mainland Scotland. Many sent livestock to three Aberdeen firms such as Auctioneers Reith & Anderson Ltd. who held auctions every Friday at Kittybrewster Auction Mart in Aberdeen and regularly dealt with Orkney livestock. Another popular mart was the City Auction Mart in Aberdeen, where the long-established firm of

John Duncan & Son Ltd. held sales three times a week. The other Aberdeen firm was that of Alexander Middleton & Son Ltd., which held its sales at what it claimed was the oldest established market in the north of Scotland, Belmont Auction Mart. Further south Thomas Dickson & Sons advertised for hides, sheepskins, wool and tallow and its adverts stated that special attention and prices applied for Orkney and Shetland hides.

In February the newspapers were proudly announcing the fact that thus far only one Orcadian had registered as being a conscientious objector. The newspaper commented on this fine record while highlighting that other areas had far more objectors. The fact that the sole Orcadian objector to register came from what was described as a remote part of the county was seen as a sign of the area's fighting spirit.

On 17 February men who had been born between 2 December 1919 and 31 December 1919 and men born between 1 January 1916 and 1 December 1916 were ordered to register with the Ministry of Labour. This required them to prove their identity by producing their identity card and provide recruiting boards several pieces of information about themselves including particulars about their employment. The Ministry then checked that the details given were correct by contacting their employers. This information was used to establish whether or not a young man was in a reserved occupation, had a trade which might be usefully employed in the services, or was eligible for call-up. Young Orcadians were encouraged to ensure that they gave the correct details of their employment as using a defence claiming that details had been recorded inaccurately would not be permitted once they had been called up. In addition, there were heavy penalties for providing incorrect information.

For the men who knew they were eligible for call-up there was little choice, although they could express a preference for service in the Royal Navy or RAF as opposed to the Army. Fishermen and seaman serving in the Merchant Navy were told to present themselves at the Mercantile Marine Office instead of the Ministry of Labour, as were marine engineering apprentices and students at Wireless Telegraphy School with the intention of going to sea as radio officers.

The recruiting boards had no power to exempt people from service or to delay service except under exceptional circumstances, such as being able to provide proof of exceptional hardship. The only way out for a young man wishing to avoid service was to hope they failed the medical examination or to declare themselves as a conscientious objector and appear before a tribunal board to prove this.

With the extensive naval facilities on Orkney the blackout regulations were rigorously enforced and Orkney Sheriff's Court heard a case on 12 March which involved a naval officer who was accused of breaching the blackout regulations. Somewhat unusually the accused remained anonymous and was referred to only as a Paymaster Captain, RN. It was alleged that the accused had gone upstairs in his Cromwell Road lodging house and had subsequently forgotten to turn off an upstairs light. Two constables had noticed the light from the pier. At first they believed, due to the brightness, that the light must be momentary but three-quarters of an hour later the light was still visible and the constables had gone to investigate, establishing that it came from Harbourview, Cromwell Road. They then spoke to the owner of the house who told them that it was a lodger's room, that he had black-out material and that she had had cause to complain to him on previous occasions about his laxity in blacking out his rooms, with little effect.

The two officers then spoke to the Paymaster Captain only for him to attempt to 'use his position to overawe the police and had threatened to report them to the Chief Constable, and actually had complained to the Chief Constable'. His solicitor said on behalf of the accused that he had forgotten to extinguish the light and that he felt the pressure of his position very much. The bench confirmed that the accused's landlady had complained of his failure to comply with the blackout on several previous occasions and, saying that he should have known better, fined the Paymaster Captain the sum of £3. In this, the bench would seem to have been particularly lenient as the possible penalties were a fine of up to £100, three months' imprisonment or a fine and imprisonment.

Amongst the charitable collections which were concerning the people of Orkney at this time was a fund set up for the aid of Finland. By the middle of March the Finland Fund stood at £553 8s.

As dusk fell on the evening of Saturday 16 March the Luftwaffe once again attacked Scapa Flow. This was the largest air raid on British soil so far in the war with at least fourteen aircraft taking part in the raid which targeted both naval units and military installations. HMS *Norfolk* was struck by at least one bomb which resulted in four deaths and three injured.[12] The cruiser was damaged badly enough to require repairs. The press reported that no military facilities on Orkney were hit despite 'the hundreds of bombs dropped'.

One of the many barrage balloons used to protect Orkney and Scapa Flow. (Public Domain)

The inaccuracy of the bombing resulted in the first civilian fatality on British soil as a result of enemy action during the war, while a further five civilians were injured and there was substantial civilian property damage across Orkney. The civilian casualties happened in the Stenness area with five of the six casualties occurring at a cluster of cottages on the Kirkwall side of the Bridge of Waithe, beside the junction of the Orphir road and the main Kirkwall-Stromness road, while the other casualty, James Jamieson, occurred at Bankburn. Several of the residents had come out to their doorways to watch the bombing over Scapa Flow and the fierce anti-aircraft fire which was being directed at the raiders when a cluster of bombs fell across the road from them. Mr James William Isbister (27), a council worker, was one of those who was watching the raid. As a result of the bombs exploding just across the road from the cottages, Mr Isbister was hit by pieces of shrapnel and splinters and died within moments. Even more tragically, Mr Isbister's wife of just two years, Lilian Fraser Tait Isbister, and his eight-month-old son were inside the cottage and witnessed his death, although they were uninjured. The casualties are shown below.

Civilian Casualties of Air Raid on 16 March 1940.

Name	Age	Injuries
William Farquhar	44	Multiple wounds to wrist and back from shrapnel.
James William Isbister	27	Fatality as a result of shrapnel injuries.
James Jamieson	65	Compound fracture of femur as a result of bomb splinter.
Alfred Garson Linklater	35	Injury to left side from shrapnel.
Miss Isa McLeod	56	Injuries to right thigh and back from shrapnel.
Mrs Jane Jessie Muir	64	Injuries to thighs and back from shrapnel.

Miss McLeod had a particularly fortunate escape as four bombs fell not more than five yards from her cottage, resulting in the building being almost demolished with only a skeleton remaining. Miss McLeod, who lived there alone, managed to extricate herself from the wreckage unaided despite her injuries. All of the cottages were damaged to some extent and in a nearby hen house all of the poultry were killed by concussive blast. The damage to the cottages was so severe that none of the residents could remain in them overnight and they instead found shelter at neighbouring farms. Two farms at Stenness also received damage, largely through incendiary bombs. At one of these the farmer, Mr James Donaldson, and his family successfully fought a fire which had been started by an incendiary bomb falling on a shed. Showing great courage and fortitude, the Donaldson family fought the fire while the raid continued around them.

Private Robert Linder was also injured in the Stenness area as a result of the raid. He was riding a motorcycle and collided with a car after a bomb fell nearby. Private Linder suffered a laceration to his left thigh as a result of the collision.

Damage to cottages at Bridge of Waite. (The Sphere)

Aircraftman Hugh Stewart was wounded in the left cheek by a piece of shrapnel at Craigiefield.

Craigiefield House, the residence of Captain Work and his wife, was damaged when several bombs dropped in the vicinity and incendiary bombs, which fell in the garden, set fire to two trees. The Graemeshall home of Orkney's assistant ARP Controller, Mr P.N. Sutherland-Graeme, had twenty-six windows blown in by blast and his gardener, Andrew Strout, had a lucky escape when a bomb exploded between his cottage and the hall resulting in damage to his cottage. Some of the raiders also strafed the area and it was reported that one woman in Orphir received slight injuries as a result of a glancing machine-gun bullet which entered her home through the porch.

Orkney's ARP organizations had undergone an extensive exercise just a fortnight before the raid and thus were as prepared as they could be for the real thing. The organization coped well. As reports of casualties and damage began to come into the centre at Kirkwall, the organization swung smoothly into action with first aid squads, repair squads and units from the fire brigade being dispatched to areas which had reported in. Two ambulances were sent to Stenness and one to Craigiehall with the injured being brought to Balfour Hospital, Kirkwall. Men from the ARP services were also dispatched to all areas of the mainland where bombs had been seen to fall.

There were, however, criticisms of the lack of warning before the raid with the sirens only sounding several minutes after it started. Many of the people of Kirkwall exhibited little fear as they took to the streets to watch the flights of bombers as they swept low over their targets. Flashes and the crump of bombs were observed and heard in the direction of Scapa and the pale fingers of searchlights and the criss-cross patterns of tracer fire provided talking points. As the raid became more severe over Kirkwall, however, the crowds took to the shelters. It was noted that although there was no sign of panic, some young children who were caught out in the raid were badly frightened. Other

Kirkwall residents took a more sanguine view. At the Temperance Hall an audience of several hundred were watching an amateur dramatics performance and remained seated despite the raid. At the Albert Kinema the feature, ironically a thriller set in the air, was briefly interrupted as the audience were informed of the raid and told that they did not have to leave if they did not wish to. No-one did.

Assessments of the raid in the period immediately following its end came to the conclusion that over 100 high-explosive bombs and approximately 400 incendiary bombs were dropped on the mainland alone. This did not include the bombs which were dropped on naval units at Scapa Flow. Sixty-seven bombs were dropped on Stenness along with 200 incendiaries; 14 bombs and 50 incendiaries were dropped at Craigiefield and 12 high-explosive bombs were dropped at Crossiecrown; 100 incendiaries fell in Kirkwall Bay, a single bomb and approximately 120 incendiaries were dropped at New Holland, Holm and between St Mary's Village, Holm, and in Graemeshall 19 bombs were dropped. People at Finstown, Sandwick and Birsay reported seeing an enemy bomber flying very low which appeared badly damaged and it was later confirmed by the Admiralty that one of the raiders had been shot down and two more damaged.

The raid and particularly the fact that one of their own had been killed, elicited a mixture of excitement and curiosity amongst many residents. On Sunday morning hundreds of people journeyed to Bridge of Waithe to view the damaged cottages where the tragedy had occurred. So heavy was the traffic that a constable from Stromness had to direct it. The cottage of Miss McLeod drew the most attention as it was practically shattered by the concussion of so many very near misses. The cottage of the unfortunate Mr Isbister and a neighbouring property were also badly damaged and all of the cottages in the group had suffered smashed windows and less serious damage. The many bomb craters in the fields surrounding the cottages also proved an attraction, with many Orcadians scouring them in the hope of obtaining a bomb splinter as a souvenir. Craigiehall and the areas of Holm which had been bombed also attracted large numbers of souvenir hunters and sightseers.

For the stunned residents of Stenness there was little to be excited about. Mr John Isbister, a blacksmith and son of a farmer and the brother-in-law of the man who was killed, described the night's events to the *Orkney Herald*. Describing it as an evening which he would never forget, he told the reporter that 'it is difficult for us to realise that such terrible things have been happening in Stenness'. Mr Isbister described how his first intimation of the raid came at around 8pm when he heard the unmistakable sound of German aircraft. Stepping out of his home he immediately saw a German bomber pass low overhead and saw and heard anti-aircraft fire from the direction of Scapa. After a time the firing slackened off somewhat and Mr Isbister, believing the raid was passing, went down to check on his workshop at Bridge of Waithe. As he passed the cottages he noticed that some of the residents had come out to watch the raid and they exchanged remarks 'about it being an exciting night'. Suddenly the firing grew more intensive and Mr Isbiston went back to his farm at Upper Onston, a few hundred yards from Bridge of Waithe. He had only just made it back under cover when he heard aircraft once more. Shortly afterwards there was a series of loud explosions quite close by and he observed flashes of fire through the windows. At the neighbouring farm of Queena several haystacks caught fire after being hit by incendiaries. Seconds later there were a series of explosions which sounded as if they were just outside and which 'shook the house to its foundations' and caused the children to scream.

After the noise of aircraft grew fainter Mr Isbister once more went down to Bridge of Waithe and was shocked by the chaos and destruction which the bombs had visited upon the small community. The injured were already being seen to by neighbours when he arrived and he described that there was little fuss as everyone 'seemed to be stunned by the calamity'. After making enquiries about his brother-in-law and his family he was informed that he had been hit and killed by a splinter.

Further eye-witness accounts emerged in the immediate aftermath and one, given by a farmworker, Mr John Flett, graphically described the raid and the impact of the bombs at Bridge of Waithe. Mr Flett had been in Stromness when the raid began, but thought that it might be safer to get outside the town and into the surrounding countryside and therefore set off on his bicycle. He also described the lull in the action followed by a resumption as he was approaching the aerodrome at Howe. When just outside Bridge of Waithe he saw several aircraft in the light of a searchlight and observed a line of incendiary bombs falling in a line towards him. There was then a number of shattering explosions and Mr Flett, admitting that he felt a momentary flash of panic, threw himself from his bike into a roadside ditch. There were several more explosions and Mr Flett described clods, divots and stones landing on the road like hail. He was himself struck by several clods as he sheltered in the ditch. One bomb made such a din that he believed it might have fallen within 10 yards but must have been more like 50 yards. Mr Flett admitted, 'Anyway, it was a bit too close for my liking'.

After the raid seemed to have passed Mr Flett got out of the ditch and made his way quickly by bicycle to the cottages of Bridge of Waithe to see if he could help. Approaching the rear of the cottages on foot he fell into a bomb crater but was able to scramble out. He then reached the cottage which had been most damaged. He described the cottage as still standing but with massive damage, the roof torn off, plaster and brickwork crumbling and falling, and a pile of debris at the front entrance. A man then grabbed his arm and shouted that there was 'a wife in that hoose'. Mr Flett and two other men were attempting to gain entrance to the cottage when Miss McLeod appeared and they were able to help her from her ruined cottage. Mr Flett said that in his opinion it was a miracle that she survived as most of the roof had fallen in on her but despite her obvious injuries Miss McLeod, when asked if she was hurt, simply replied 'No so bad'.[13]

Mr Flett then went to see if he could assist with any of the injured and described how people reacted very bravely. When he asked one of the other men on the scene if anyone had been seriously hurt he was told that Mr Isbister had been killed. Attempts to summon help were somewhat hindered by the fact that the bombs had brought down the telephone wires but ambulances and first aid squads soon arrived.

In the hours and days following the raid the people of Stenness showed a great deal of sympathy towards the widow of Mr Isbister and to his wider family at Upper Onston. The victim had been a very popular man and was well known in both Kirkwall and Stromness.

One area in which the authorities faced criticism was in the slow reporting of the incident which, once more, allowed the German propaganda machine to get its own, highly exaggerated, side of the story in first. A press conference was held in Germany at which airmen who had flown on the raid spoke. The commander of the squadron stated that direct hits had been scored on HMS *Hood*, HMS *Repulse* and HMS *Renown*, along with an unnamed cruiser. The Germans believed that all these ships, had been seriously damaged. In fact, barring the cruiser HMS *Norfolk*, no other naval craft was hit.[14] The German authorities also claimed that they had successfully attacked aerodromes at Stromness, Earth House and Kirkwall as well as anti-aircraft positions. The German account of the attack was put out over the radio at 3am and it was not until after midday on the Sunday that the British authorities announced the news.

The story of the amateur dramatics at the Temperance Hall during the bombing raid quickly went around Orkney and the local press took up the story. The play was the final night of a short run of 'Tilly of Bloomsbury' by the Kirkwall Amateur Dramatics Society and was described as having been an even better performance than the previous night's despite the bombing going on a short distance away. A large audience, including many servicemen, was in attendance and the only people who left were a couple of air raid wardens who had to attend to their duties. Late arrivals were astonished to find that the performance had not been cancelled and that the curtain had gone up on time. Halfway through the second act Lieutenant Davis of Kirkwall Naval Base interrupted to inform the performers and audience that although a raid had been going on the all-clear had now sounded and they could continue uninterrupted. The production had been under the auspices of the Kirkwall Naval Base Sports Club and the proceeds from the four-day tour were given to that group and to the RNLI and the Shipwrecked Mariners' Society.

Along with the Orkney Direct Line ships, services were provided by the mail aircraft of Scottish Airways. On the morning of 19 March there was a potentially fatal incident involving one of their de Haviland Dragon Rapide aircraft when it crashed on take-off from Wideford civil aerodrome. The Rapide was carrying a pilot and six passengers bound for Inverness but failed to gain altitude, clipped a stone wall and crashed through two fences before coming to rest having spun through 180 degrees. The pilot and passengers hurriedly extricated themselves and managed to salvage the mails even though the aircraft had quickly burst into flames.

The Luftwaffe made two more attempts to raid Scapa Flow on 8 and 10 April. In the second raid the area was warned when the sirens sounded shortly before 9pm. Although dusk was approaching the sky was very clear. The anti-aircraft batteries in the area immediately began firing, but those residents looking to the skies could not see the bombers as they were too high. The RAF and the anti-aircraft batteries claimed to have shot down seven bombers and to have badly damaged at least two more out of what was claimed to have been a force of sixty aircraft in four waves. Once more no damage was done and injuries were limited to one serviceman who received a slight wound from a machine-gun bullet. Although the German bombers dropped a large number of bombs they were met with a ferocious anti-aircraft barrage, which forced them to such a height that their accuracy was seriously impinged.

Several of the raiders broke through the barrage and descended to a lower height from which they strafed targets in the vicinity of Stromness and Kirkwall. There were claims that the Germans had deliberately strafed houses in the two communities, but this was quickly disproved. Some properties in Stromness did receive slight damage from stray rounds, but the machine-gun bullet cases which were used as evidence in several Kirkwall streets were from an aerial battle between a bomber and RAF fighters. Several Kirkwall residents witnessed a Heinkel He 111 dive steeply over the town, hotly pursued by RAF fighters. The raid lasted for approximately an hour and it was fully dark by the time it ended. Observers in Orphir and the South Isles saw two enemy aircraft caught in searchlight beams and fall apparently out of control as if they had been hit by anti-aircraft fire. At 10.30pm the raid was over and the all-clear sounded.

The third day of May brought the death of yet another Orcadian seaman. Able Seaman Gillies Harcus (19) was from Eday, the son of Peter and Jessie Arm Harcus. He was serving aboard the destroyer HMS *Afridi* and on 1 May the ship was part of the attempt to evacuate 12,000 British and French troops from central Norway following the abortive attempt to take Trondheim. After picking up and transferring troops on 2 May, HMS *Afridi* picked up more men of the York and Lancaster Regiment. *Afridi*, under the command of Captain Vian, remained at the dock waiting for the 36-man rearguard before finally casting off and making for the rest of the fleet, bound for Shetland. Under frequent air attack, the convoy took evasive action but around 10am the French destroyer *Bison* received a direct hit and began to sink. HMS *Afridi*, joined by HMS *Grenade* and HMS *Imperial*, went alongside to evacuate survivors with *Afridi* remaining behind to sink the stricken destroyer with gunfire despite further air attacks.

After rejoining the convoy HMS *Afridi* once more came under attack. Ju 87 Stuka dive-bombers attacked from both sides and the destroyer was hit by two bombs. These caused massive damage and a severe fire and it was clear that the Tribal-class destroyer's time was up. HMS *Griffin* and HMS *Imperial* came alongside, port and starboard, to take on board survivors, including Captain Vian, but at 2.45pm HMS *Afridi* capsized and sank taking with her 53 of her company, including Able Seaman Harcus, 35 of the 69 French servicemen taken aboard from *Bison*, and 13 British soldiers (the only ones out of the 12,000 evacuated from Andalsnes and Namsos to lose their lives).[15]

In response to the sinking of the HMS *Royal Oak*, Winston Churchill, in his capacity as First Lord of the Admiralty, had ordered the construction of four concrete barriers on Orkney in order to prevent submarines from penetrating the mooring. These barriers were to link the Mainland to South Ronaldsay via Burray, along with the two islands of Glimps Holm and Lamb Holm. By May the firm which had won the contract, Balfour

A Churchill Barrier.

One of the block ships used to block access to Scapa Flow. (Irene Moore)

Beatty, was ready to undertake the preparatory work on what was a huge engineering project. In order to undertake the work quarries on Orkney were required to produce 250,000 tons of rock to fill the gabions which were to be used as the base for the barriers. Overhead cableways had to be set up over the paths of the barriers so that the gabions could be dropped into place in water which in places was up to 59ft deep. In order to begin even this preparatory work a huge workforce had to be settled in Orkney and numerous hotels, guest houses and properties were used to house these workers while camps were also set up on the islands.

The second of Orkney's proposed four airfields was RAF Skeabrae. Work had started in December 1939 and by May the airfield was officially completed and declared operational. With the situation facing Britain, however, there were no RAF fighter aircraft available for the base and, in the meantime, it had to make do with the outdated aircraft of the Fleet Air Arm (FAA). The aircraft available for the immediate defence of Scapa Flow included the Sea Gladiator and Blackburn Roc fighters (both of which were obsolete), the Fairey Fulmar (again outperformed by modern fighters) and the Blackburn Skua fighter-dive bomber (which was obsolescent).

In mid-June the Secretary of State for War announced that, due to military exigencies, Orkney and Shetland would henceforth be placed under curfew. This made it an offence for

Gloster Gladiator (similar to a Sea Gladiator). (Public Domain)

Blackburn Roc. (Public Domain)

anyone to be outside after 11pm without the permission of the relevant authorities. Primarily the curfew meant that people on Orkney could not travel, be outdoors, or be near to a road after the curfew hour without the permission of an Army, RN, RAF or police officer. Penalties for breaching the curfew, which

Fairey Fulmar. (Public Domain)

Blackburn Skua fighter-dive bomber. (Public Domain)

were enforced under the Defence Regulations, included fines not exceeding £100, imprisonment of up to three months or a fine and imprisonment. Many on the islands were left somewhat bewildered and uneasy at this announcement as it would mean a severe restriction in the many social activities which had always been a traditional way of life there. Foremost amongst the worries was that, if the war was not over by the New Year, then Hogmanay was going to be a particularly dismal affair for the inhabitants of the protected area.

We have already seen how a strict curfew was put in place on Orkney (and Shetland). Due to problems of advertising the curfew it was not strictly enforced until 15 July and on the next day the first prosecution under this new law came before Orkney Sheriff's Court. The accused was a Mr James Campbell (44), a marine engineer employed on a drifter at Holm. Mr Campbell had gotten drunk in Kirkwall on the night of 15 July and at approximately 2.30am on 16 July was found wandering on the Kirkwall–Deerness road and taken into custody by the military when he admitted having no permit to break curfew. Mr Campbell pleaded guilty to the charge and offered no defence for his behaviour (he represented himself). From the bench, Sheriff Brown said that, as this was the first prosecution under the new law, he was apt to be lenient and gave Campbell one week to pay a fine of £1 or face ten days imprisonment. The curfew was, of course, unpopular with many Orcadians who felt that it unnecessarily curtailed social life on the islands and this seems to have been reflected in some aspects of this first prosecution. As revealed above, the Sheriff appeared reluctant to impose too severe a penalty and the *Orkney Herald* ran the article under the headline 'First "Victim" of Orkney Curfew', clearly signalling some sympathy with the unfortunate Mr Campbell.[16]

The strategic importance of Orkney, however, was made abundantly clear in an article on the same page which related the details of the above court case. The Admiralty announced that a huge new mine belt had been laid between Orkney and Ireland, and Iceland and Greenland, forcing any shipping traffic between the Atlantic and the northern European nations to converge upon the port of Kirkwall. Any vessels which wished to continue on to the northern European ports would have to travel through the Pentland Firth to Kirkwall where they would receive further instructions. Likewise, vessels travelling from Russian or Finnish ports to the Atlantic were ordered to proceed to Kirkwall for instructions. Masters of these vessels were warned that they ignored such instructions and routing at their own peril.

The Women's Voluntary Service (WVS) was continuing its sterling knitting campaign to provide comforts for British servicemen. Despite the fine summer weather the women of Orkney's WVS work parties continued to demand wool and material so that they could put their skills to use in aid of the war effort and a fine stock was being laid up for the colder months when servicemen would no doubt be glad of warm garments. The organisers were particularly pleased that the effort was being maintained during the summer months and even more so by the contribution of women employed on Orkney's farms, who continued to supply large numbers of socks despite the shortages of farm labour which required them to work longer hours on the farms. Socks were particularly popular items and large numbers continued to be issued throughout the summer months. Monetary donations and donations of items of clothing which had been purchased were also made to the comforts campaign. In June there had been six monetary donations from Orkney residents which totalled over £20.

Monetary Donations to the Comforts Fund in June

Donor			
Per Miss Rosie, Holm		16s	
B.Y. & H. per Mrs McLean	£2	6s	
Misses Stewart		10s	
Anonymous	£1		
Burray door-to-door collection per Mrs Park	£8	6s	
North Ronoldsay door-to-door collection per Mrs Gordon	£7	14s	
Total	£20	12s	0d

The Orkney WVS also made a substantial contribution to the Red Cross efforts and a Sphagnum Moss Committee was set up to organise the collection, drying and distribution of the moss to the Red Cross Depot at Kirkwall. It had been rediscovered in the First World War just how effective sphagnum moss dressings were in binding wounds. The moss, when dried, is incredibly absorbent and can hold approximately twenty times its own weight in liquid; the acidity of the moss was also effective in preventing bacterial infection. Several work parties had been organized and appeals were frequently put out throughout the summer as the weather was perfect for drying the moss. Where work parties were not immediately available people, almost always women, were urged to collect, dry and clean the moss and send it to the Red Cross depot in clean sacks. Those who wished to make their own dressings without the aid of a work party could be sent muslin by appealing to the Red Cross depot.

With the Battle of Britain raging the press hammered home the point made by Lord Beaverbrook that more aircraft were required for the nation's war effort. In his capacity as Minister for Aircraft Production Lord Beaverbrook urgently asked for the general public and local authorities to donate metals, especially aluminium, for use in the manufacture of aircraft. Telling the British public that no contribution was too humble and that they would 'turn your pots and pans into Hurricanes and Spitfires', Lord Beaverbrook ensured that the campaign took root in the British psyche. On Orkney the collection of aluminium items was organized once more by the local branch of the WVS. Weekly collections were held at Kirkwall Grammar School every Monday and Thursday from 2.30 to 4.30pm. The chief WVS organizer on Orkney, the aptly named Mrs Work, told the local press that there had been many enquiries as to whether a collection scheme would be organized on the islands and that, as a result, the WVS had stepped in to organize it. For those outside Kirkwall who wished to contribute, Mrs Work instructed them to send their contributions to the school in sacks and it was believed that free transport would be given to donations by local bus and steamer companies.

Late July also brought news of more rationing to add to the difficulties of the Orcadian housewife. From 22 July margarine was also brought onto the ration and housewives were told that if they were already registered with a retailer for their butter ration then they need take no further action, but that if they were not already registered then they should register with a suitable retailer immediately. Some Orcadians preferred to register for their butter supply direct from local farmers and they were assured that they would be able to collect their 6oz weekly butter ration in farm butter from 22 July. In order to prevent those private individuals who kept poultry from profiteering through the selling of surplus eggs whilst still making a profit, the Ministry of Food also issued an order in July which fixed maximum prices for the sale of home-produced eggs. The prices were divided according to category but had to conform to the individual weight standards which had been issued previously.

Home-Produced Eggs, Maximum Prices (per dozen)

Category		
1A	2s	9d
1B	2s	6d
1C	2s	3d
1D	2s	

There was some relief, however, as everyone with a ration card was informed that they could draw an extra ration of 2lbs of sugar during July as long as the sugar was only used for the purpose of preserving fruit. Thus, for example, a family of four would be entitled to receive an extra 8lbs of sugar for jam making or the bottling of fruit. Although the majority of housewives were considering jam-making they were urged instead to consider bottling fruit as it was the best way of preserving large stocks of precious fruit for long-term use. In order to aid the housewife who was considering bottling fruit for the first time, the Ministry of Agriculture published a pamphlet, costing 4d, entitled 'Preserves from the Garden'. The pamphlet included complete and concise instructions on the making of jams and jellies, the bottling, canning and pulping of fruit, the drying of fruit and vegetables and recipes for the preparation of chutneys, pickles, fruit cheeses and so on. The pamphlet also gave full instructions for the preparation of jars suitable for preserving.

Although Orkney had already been raided, arrangements had only just been made to give instructions to the local residents on first aid skills which might be required to render immediate aid to victims of enemy action. The Medical Officer of the county, Dr Bannerman, had arranged for a series of eight lectures which took place at the Kirkwall Congregational Church. The first lecture was given by Dr John Tait, Professor of Physiology at McGill University, Montreal. An audience of sixty or so people attended the first lecture and the speaker was warmly welcomed. The three-quarter hour lecture was very well received, with Dr Tait telling the audience that the main issues to be dealt with included fainting, haemorrhage, various types of wounds and shock. There was considerable enthusiasm when Dr Tait organized the second lecture a week later. In addition to the lectures, twice weekly demonstration meetings were also introduced, under Dr Gunn, and this meant that the entire course could be completed within a month.

The third of Orkney's airfields was opened in August as RAF Grimsetter (also known as RAF Kirkwall). This was a sector operations room and gunnery control room and was used initially as a satellite and relief airfield. It was later transferred to control of, first, the FAA as HMS *Robin* and then back to the RAF.

Orkney was a relative latecomer to the phenomena of the Spitfire Fund. The community-driven efforts to fund the building of and to sponsor one of the iconic fighter aircraft had begun elsewhere as early as May and had proved immensely popular. By August the *Orkney Herald* was reporting that there had been a large number of enquiries as to whether a fund would be started on Orkney. The newspaper itself exerted additional pressure in support of such a campaign by running an article under the headline 'Orcadians want a Spitfire Fund'. Readers were informed that while no fund was in place it seemed a 'certainty that the establishment of such a fund cannot be long delayed'. The newspaper argued that the will was there amongst Orcadians but all that was lacking was a suitable organizer. Surely, the paper argued, if Orcadians could contribute £200,000 to the National Savings Campaign, they would have no problem in raising the £5,000 required to purchase a Spitfire for Orkney.

The enthusiasm for such a fund was reflected in the number of people who had already stated they would contribute. These included James McDonald, a butcher from Albert Street in Kirkwall, who promised that he and other members of his family were willing and ready to contribute £100. On 15 August the West Mainland Agricultural Society had a meeting at Dounby at which it was decided to hold sheep-dog trials in aid of the, as yet to be formed, Orkney Spitfire Fund. The secretary of the society, Mr James Wood of Garson, Sandwick, told the newspaper that the support for the project was unanimous and that while they sincerely hoped that the fund would become a reality if it did not then the funds would be donated to various war charities. Mr Wood said that the show would mean 'Southerners will discover what the people of Orkney have long realised, that as a form of outdoor entertainment sheep-dog trials have few equals', but that the most important consideration would be 'that all who support the event will be helping the RAF to blow Hitler's bombers out of the sky'.[17] The newspaper even made the suggestion that the society itself might put themselves forward as organizers of the fund.

The August meeting of the St Ola branch of the Women's Royal Institute (WRI) had the subject of vegetable cooking as its main theme. The president read a paper containing many useful hints for cooking with vegetables and Mrs Harcus of Glaitness Farm presented her recipe for vegetable pie. Other subjects covered during the meeting included the collection of garden flowers and a competition was held for the best arrangement, won by Mrs Twatt. The meeting, held at Kirkwall Grammar School, also featured a delicious tea for the many attendees and collections of socks, hospital cushions, bags and paper were handed in.

Although the vast majority of sailors who passed through Orkney were well behaved and did not trouble the residents, there were exceptions. On 23 August Orkney Sheriff Court heard the case of two men, William Mann (stoker) and William Raigan (seaman), who were accused of having banged on doors at Crantit House, St Ola, smashed six panes of glass at the house and 'shouted and bawled, conducted themselves in a riotous and disorderly manner'. The two men did not have any representative and pleaded guilty to the charges. Sheriff Brown fined the men £2 with two months to pay or face fourteen days in prison.

The end of the month brought news that another Burray resident had been killed. Alistair St Clair Duncan (28) was the Second Officer aboard the SS *Anglo-Saxon* and lost his life when the cargo ship was sunk by the German auxiliary cruiser and merchant raider *Widder*. The British merchantman had been steaming from Wales to Argentina with a cargo of coal when she came under fire from the *Widder* on the night of 21 August. The first barrage consisted of 150mm shells which hit the poop deck and aft gun platform, detonating the shells there and killing most of the crew who were in the forecastle. The *Widder* then closed on the stricken merchant ship and opened up a furious barrage of 150mm shells along with 37mm and 20mm cannons. This barrage killed more of the crew, holed the lifeboats which the survivors were attempting to launch and destroyed the radio room, preventing any distress call from being sent. A further salvo of 150mm shells then exploded the boiler and the *Widder* launched a torpedo which struck the *Anglo-Saxon* and caused her to sink very quickly. Two lifeboats were launched while seven survivors climbed into a jolly boat. Eyewitnesses later reported that the *Widder* had deliberately machine-gunned those in the two lifeboats and in the water before steaming off without trying to pick up survivors.[18]

SS Anglo-Saxon. *(Public Domain)*

Alistair St Clair Duncan was an only son who lived with his mother (his father, a police constable, had died before 1936) at Westshore, Burray, and was an experienced seaman having earned his mate's ticket at Glasgow in 1936. He is commemorated on the Tower Hill Memorial.

For the many sailors from the Royal Navy who were present in Orkney the war could often seem far away and the authorities were well aware that if morale was to be maintained there was a need for relatively substantial facilities for relaxation. One establishment which provided a warm welcome to all members of the forces was the Toc-H and Pilgrim Trust convalescent home at Woodwick, Evie. Towards the end of August a party of sailors from the Home Fleet visited the home at an opportune moment when one of the original founders of the original Toc-H rest centre, the Reverend Phillip Thomas Byard 'Tubby' Clayton CH MC, was present. The group took the opportunity to have a group photograph taken with themselves, the Reverend and the Toc-H, Orkney, mascot, a cocker spaniel named 'Billy' which had been a gift from Queen Mary to replace 'Tubby' Clayton's

A cheery party from the Fleet visiting Woodwick Convalescent Home, Evie, established by Toc H and Pilgrim Trust. " Billy " the cocker spaniel, a gift of H.M. Queen Mary to Toc H, Orkney, is seen with Rev. " Tubby " Clayton, founder padre of Toc H.

Sailors with The Rev. Tubby Clayton (holding 'Billy') during a visit to the Woodwick Convalescent Home. (Orkney Herald)

previous cocker spaniel, 'Smuts', which had been killed in an air raid on Orkney during the previous October.

Cinema remained a key attraction for people looking for some relaxation during the war. Kirkwall had just one cinema, the Albert Kinema, and in August this was offering such treats as romantic drama 'Escape to Happiness' starring Leslie Howard and Ingrid Bergman but the most popular feature was undoubtedly 'Tarzan finds a Son' starring Johnny Weissmuller.

As the wartime situation became ever more serious more food items were added to the list of those whose prices were controlled by the government. The Canned Milk Order was introduced, for example, on 4 September. The order prescribed the maximum prices which could be charged for different varieties of canned milk. The new prices resulted in an increase of 1d for large cans and ½d for small cans of special full cream sweetened milk, an increase of ½d and ¼d respectively for large and small cans of full cream sweetened milk but a decrease of ¼d for the largest tins of skimmed condensed milk. The order did not just affect those who were buying and selling canned milk, but also those who were purchasing the product for ship's stores or for the production of various foods. The special full cream unsweetened milk which was available only for use in ship's stores was also regulated by the order. So as to control the product with regard to those who were purchasing it for use in food production, the Condensed Milk (Bulk) Order came into force on 9 September and controlled prices for bulk purchases.

Canned Milk Price List

Product	Price
Special Full Cream Sweetened (large)	11d
Special Full Cream Sweetened (small)	5¾d
Full Cream Sweetened (large)	9¾d
Full Cream Sweetened (small)	5¼d
Full Cream Unsweetened (large)	8d
Full Cream Unsweetened (small)	3¾d
Skimmed (large)	6d
Skimmed (medium)	5d
Skimmed (small)	4d

Despite the fact that Britain was facing a crisis of unprecedented proportions, there were some who were still committing crimes for their own profit regardless of the national situation. On 17 September a case was heard at Orkney Sheriff Court regarding a theft which had occurred just days before war had been declared. The accused was a camp cook named Robert McPherson (40) who was employed by contractors at a camp in the North Isles. At the end of August he was journeying to Kirkwall aboard the steamer *Earl Sigurd* with a fellow cook, James Firth Walter. In the course of the journey the two men had gone ashore at

Stronsay and drank together before returning to the steamer and playing bridge for some considerable time. Walter lost the game and produced his wallet, which contained £55, and paid Mr McPherson the sum of £2 before he then fell asleep.

Mr Walter did not awaken until two hours after the steamer had docked at Kirkwall and quickly realised that his wallet was missing. Upon going ashore, he immediately reported the theft to the police and declared his suspicions of Mr McPherson, whom he knew only possessed the £2 he had paid him. Police investigations quickly revealed that after going ashore Mr McPherson had purchased new clothes to the value of £4 3s 6d and, when he was arrested the next morning, he was found to have the sum of £50 1s 4½d in his possession.

Sheriff Brown heard how Mr McPherson was a widower with one child and the Fiscal stated that he had seventeen previous convictions against him for dishonest appropriation. Mr McPherson's defence stated that Mr Walter had been very drunk and that McPherson had seen him drop his wallet and had picked it up with the intention of returning the wallet when Mr Walter sobered up, but he had been arrested before he had the chance.

Sheriff Brown was having none of it and, stating that Mr McPherson's criminal past was part of a lamentable record and that previous leniency which had been shown to him had been completely ineffective, immediately sentenced him to nine months' imprisonment.

By October 804 Squadron at RAF Skeabrae received a much more potent fighter in the Martlet I. This was an American fighter aircraft, designated the Grumman F4F Wildcat in US service, and was a far more advanced fighter than those previously available. It was still outmatched by modern German fighters such as the Messerschmitt Me 109, but was more than a match for the bombers it would face over Orkney.

In mid-October the Orkney Spitfire Fund was able to donate the sum of £6,800 to the Ministry of Aircraft Production, and a Spitfire IIB, P8344, was duly christened 'Orkney'. The fighter

A Martlet I (Grumman F4F Wildcat) of the FAA. (Public Domain)

went on to serve with at least five separate RAF squadrons[19] and the Lord Lieutenant of Orkney and Shetland, Mr Alfred Baikie of Tankerness, received a letter of thanks for the contribution from Lord Beaverbrook.

By the end of the month some people were querying the attitude of certain Orcadians towards the fund-raising efforts for the newly renamed Orkney Fighter Fund (it had been decided to purchase a Hurricane to go along with the Spitfire). One man, signing himself simply as 'Critic' wrote to the *Orkney Herald* claiming that although the sum raised was higher than that of neighbouring areas such as Shetland and Caithness, there was disappointment that those neighbouring areas had a wider range of donors compared to Orkney's efforts. The writer claimed that if greater number of Orcadians had contributed to the fund then an extra £2,000 would have been added to the £7,000 already raised. The fundraising on Orkney had been marked by smaller numbers of donors giving larger sums. While the writer praised those who had made a contribution, he had noticed that, in the published lists of donors, there were 'many absent names, prominent merchants and leading citizens in town and country districts'.[20] Furthermore, the donations had tailed off after the enthusiastic start and in the last week of October only £83 had been given.

The writer went on to criticise the self-satisfaction that was evident amongst some Orcadians with regard to the fund, stating that the county's reserves were far from exhausted but that little was being done to organise collections or to organise events in support of the fund. He also queried whether greater efforts could be made by those who were present on Orkney due to the war. He admitted that the services had already made a worthwhile contribution to the fund but that league tables published in newspapers which compared the efforts of various parts of Scotland failed to take into account the fact that Orkney's population had increased substantially as a result of the war.

Stromness welcomes the men of a Highland Regiment. (Public Domain)

Servicewomen at Stromness. (Unknown)

Oddly, not everyone had been or remained a fan of the Orkney Fighter Fund, with one letter appearing to criticise the fundraising attempts in November. The writer, J. Creagh Scott, claimed that the Spitfire funds were either a humbug or that the government was unwilling to pay for aircraft themselves. The government, he claimed, could not have it both ways. Showing his contempt for the fundraising attempts he said that the 'unending appeals for this and other funds are either complete humbug – which they are' before saying that 'these well-intentioned but unofficial tax collections will not, obviously, produce a single more Spitfire or bomber'.[21] After describing the Spitfire Funds as 'a tragic mixture of hysteria and economic lunacy', he concluded by challenging anyone to tell him how war production was aided by Spitfire Funds. Lieutenant Colonel J. Creagh Scott got his answer when a number of readers of the *Orkney Herald* wrote in expressing their contempt for him and calling him a crank who was lacking patriotic spirit and clearly no friend of the government or of the war effort; in this they were quite correct.[22]

The end of October brought news that the curfew which had been in force during the hours of darkness on Orkney was to be lifted. The majority of Orcadians reacted with a sense of relief to this news but not everyone was happy. A particularly grumpy response was elicited from one man who wrote to the *Orkney Herald* expressing his disappointment in the announcement. Writing from Stromness, Mr J.E. Turner claimed that in the winter months the curfew was even welcome as it assured householders of peace and quiet from 10.30pm onwards and that it meant that householders 'when burdened by unwelcome visitors' could rely on the curfew to send them packing but, he continued, 'Now, unfortunately, we shall have the house cluttered up once again with these pests until all hours of the morning'. The writer was more seriously concerned with the fact that the raising of the curfew would mean that there would no longer be a 'check on the wanderings of the many "toughs" who have come into this county as navvies'. The writer expressed his views that things had been bad enough with the curfew but that, henceforth, the problems would increase, especially for the residents of Kirkwall, Stromness, Finstown and Dounsby. He continued by saying that the curfew had not had an impact upon the social life of Orkney as dances and other events had continued to go on but had stopped before 11pm. Mr Turner concluded by saying that to law-abiding Orcadians the curfew had been a blessing and that the raising of it would mean more work for an already pressed police force.[23]

There was a sad announcement on Christmas Day when the *Orkney Herald* revealed that Seaman John Kent Foulis (19) of Chapelbrae, Westray, had lost his life at sea due to enemy action. After leaving school, John had briefly worked on the farm at Brough before joining the Merchant Navy in 1937. He was well known on Westray and was described as being cheerful, full of life, happy and a friend to all. The newspaper extended its deepest sympathy to his parents, John and Winifred. John had been aboard the SS *Diplomat* and was sailing as part of convoy HX-88. The merchant ship, carrying 4,484 tons of cotton,

2,760 tons of iron and steel and 1,603 tons of general cargo, had fallen behind the rest of the convoy and was torpedoed and sunk by *U-104* off the coast of County Donegal. Fourteen of her 53-man crew were lost with the survivors being picked up by a British destroyer.[24]

Also on Christmas day, two Martlet I fighters of 804 Squadron intercepted a German bomber over Scapa Flow and successfully shot it down. This was the first victory in Europe of the Grumman fighter and the first for any US-built fighter in British service during the war.

Sadly, and unbeknownst to the people of Orkney, yet another merchant seaman from the islands had also lost his life in December. On 4 December Seaman Magnus Leith Henderson (34) from South Ronaldsay was part of the crew of the Walter Runciman & Co. operated MV *Empire Statesman* which was sailing in convoy. The motor merchant had fallen behind the convoy and, like the SS *Diplomat*, above, was torpedoed and sunk; 32 of her crew were lost.[25]

The *MV* Empire Statesman *when operating as the* Ansaldo VIII. *(Public Domain)*

CHAPTER 3

1941: A Losing Battle

During the second week of the New Year it was announced that Kirkwall native John Harrold had been promoted to the rank of squadron leader. The son of a retired watchmaker, Squadron Leader Harrold had been in the RAF for a considerable number of years and was, at the time of his promotion, serving in Egypt. His parents, Robert and Jean, who lived at St Catherine's Place, Kirkwall, announced the news in the local press and received many messages of congratulation from those who remembered Squadron Leader Harrold fondly.

Despite the raids of the previous year there was still some recalcitrance when it came to voluntary service with some of the ARP organizations. The first week of the year had seen an appeal from the Clerk to the Orkney County Council Emergency Committee for volunteers from Kirkwall and Stromness to serve in parties to fight incendiary bombs dropped by the enemy. Despite raids on the islands during the previous year there was a less than enthusiastic response and it was believed that not enough people in the towns realised the importance of having these fire-fighting parties readily available. The fire brigades and AFS were doing a fine job, but reinforcement in the form of volunteers were needed in what the Clerk, reflecting the words of Mr Herbert Morrison, said was a new Home Guard. Those who were interested were instructed to leave their names and contact details at Kirkwall and Stromness police stations and it was hoped that one recruit from each family would be reached.

Tragedy hit the Kelday family in the first week of the year. Mr Thomas Kelday, a farmworker employed at Weyland Farm, East Hill, Kirkwall, was returning home after an evening out with friends when he attempted to cross the Bignold Park Road. In the blackout Mr Kelday was late in seeing a lorry, but stepped back in time to avoid it only to be struck by a car travelling in the opposite direction. He suffered severe head injuries and succumbed to his wounds despite attempts to aid him. His wife had recently died and the latest tragedy to hit the family aroused a great deal of sympathy for the two sons and two daughters who survived the loss of their parents.

One of his sons, Tom, was serving on Orkney with a unit of the Royal Artillery. Mr Kelday was well known in the district and had been a respected member of the Home Guard. His funeral, held on 9 January at St Olaf's Cemetery, was of a semi-military character. A pipe band from a Highland regiment serving on Orkney played the cortège to the head of the town at a slow march while thirty Home Guardsmen marched alongside the hearse. Upon arrival at the cemetery, Mr Kelday's coffin was borne to the graveside by six Home Guardsmen from his post where a service was held and an Army bugler played the Last Post and Reveille over the grave. A great many beautiful wreaths marked the graveside showing the respect in which Mr Kelday was held by the community.[26]

The contribution made by voluntary groups to the war effort was a central plank of the wartime home front across Britain and Orkney was no different. The Scottish section of the Women's Rural Institute (WRI) was one such body. The Orkney Federation of the WRI held its summer meeting on 7 July at Kirkwall Grammar School. Miss Reid, in the chair, welcomed those attending including members from branches on Birsay, Burray, Deerness, Dounby, Harray, Holm, Orphir, Rousay, Sandwick, Shapinsay, South Ronaldsay, Stenness, St Ola, Stromness and Strongsay. Mr Barrack, manager of Orkney Savings Bank, addressed the meeting on the subject of the aims of the forthcoming War Weapons Week campaign and expressed his hope that each branch in the WRI would form a savings group and would help to enthuse their local communities. Indeed, several of the branches in the Orkney Federation had already formed groups and he expressed the hope that the others would quickly follow suit.

Moving on to other matters, the federation secretary, Miss Scarth, presented some bad news, telling members that the scheme to gather medicinal herbs was a failure. It had proved impracticable to perform the drying process on Orkney and transporting the herbs to drying centres in the south in time was impossible. Miss Scarth, however, pointed out that the WRI could continue to be of great assistance by continuing to gather sphagnum moss as it was widely used in hospitals and could be dried effectively.

After a presentation of the finances of the federation (which were described as very healthy) the meeting moved onto a short series of demonstrations on fruit bottling given by Mrs Leask of Stromness and Mrs Firth of Shapinsay. Mrs Leask demonstrated how to preserve fruit using the sterilising (boiling) technique, while Mrs Firth gave a demonstration of preserving using the oven. Mrs Firth also explained how gooseberries, rhubarb and tomatoes could all be pulped and used in tarts and similar recipes. The two demonstrators also presented a number of useful wartime recipes, amongst them were recipes for wartime lemon curd and lighthouse pudding.

Wartime Lemon Curd

Ingredients: 1 teacup of sugar; 2oz margarine; 1 cup water (or 2 cups if lemon quash is omitted); 1 cup lemon squash; 2 tablespoons lemon creamola;[27] 1 teaspoon lemon essence; 2 teaspoons tartaric acid; 1 egg.

Method:
Bring sugar, water and margarine to boil. Blend creamola with cold water and add to pan. Boil for 3 minutes. Take off heat, add lemon essence, tartaric acid, and beaten egg, stirring carefully in case it curdles. Pour into small jars and store.

Lighthouse Pudding

Ingredients: ½lb flour; ¼lb margarine or suet; ¼lb sultanas or dates; 1 large teaspoon of baking powder; pinch of salt; cold water to mix.

Method: Mix ingredients. Steam for 2-3 hours

The blitz on Clydeside, Glasgow, focused many minds throughout Scotland as the horrifying scale of the devastation and the number of casualties became clear. Amongst the many proposals aimed at relieving the suffering of those who had been bombed out, had lost loved ones, or who were vulnerable to further attacks was a campaign to evacuate the vulnerable, especially children, from Scottish cities to the Highlands and Islands. The campaign became known as the Scottish Clan Evacuation Plan and it found backing from across Scotland and abroad from many who could trace their ancestry back to Scotland. Fundraising in New York was bolstered by the efforts of Orcadian, Miss Leila McNeil.

With the national campaign for 1941 being announced as War Weapons Week, the authorities in Orkney were keen to get their own campaign organized and a public meeting was held at Kirkwall Town Hall on the evening of 8 July. The main aim of this preliminary meeting was to appoint a fully representative committee to oversee the campaign on the islands. The idea for the public meeting was the brainchild of the Lord Lieutenant of Orkney and Shetland, Mr Alfred Baikie, and he expressed the hope that the committee, once appointed, would quickly mobilise the support of every man, woman and child. War Weapons Week was a campaign to encourage war savings which the government used to purchase weapons for the pursuit of the war, and the launch of the campaign was accompanied by the publication of lists which gave the cost of various weapons that would be purchased with the funds donated. The press were keen to point out to people that the donations made to the savings campaigns were not gifts but investments, and it was hoped that

Miss McNeil (second from left) outside the Scottish Show in New York. (The Tatler)

the people of Orkney would once more show their patriotism and generosity during the week-long campaign. Mr William C. Barrack, the honorary secretary of the savings movement, pointed out that Orcadians had already contributed the sum of £418,386 2s 4d.

The meeting was very well attended with Mr Baikie in the chair and the committee was quickly selected. It included many worthies, a mix of local officials, locals with varied connections on Orkney and those with useful specialist knowledge, including Mr Barrack, the agent and manager for the Aberdeen Savings Bank, Orkney, who was appointed secretary. Mr Baikie himself was selected as chairman of the committee. The county councillors on the committee were urged to act as the driving force in their own areas. A number of sub-committees were also appointed with the aim of soliciting enthusiasm in various areas of Orkney society. These included committees for farming, shipping, banking, law, education, WVS and the Scottish Women's Rural Institute (WRI), post office, employers, employees, church and contractors. Smaller sub-committees were also enrolled for generating publicity (formed from members of the local press) and a number of members for special duties were appointed. It was agreed that representatives from the three forces would also be invited to sit on the main committee. One of the first decisions of the committee was to set a target for the week and it was decided that the aim would be for Orkney to raise the sum of £100,000.

By the end of July plans were falling into place. The campaign week was to run from 16-23 August and one of the greatest attractions were to be parades consisting of members of HM Forces, ARP and Civil Defence Services, Boys' Brigade, Boy Scouts, Girl Guides, etc. Other events included displays of fire-fighting, a sports day in Bignold Park, community singing at Market Green, music from pipe bands, displays of weaponry by all of the forces and the Home Guard in Brandyquoy Park and public addresses. Other events had been planned but, somewhat cryptically, the local press said that it could not report on these due to censorship regulations. At Stromness, Provost Marwick was working to ensure that a suitable series of events was held locally, while on the west Mainland Councillor Hourston of Beaquoy had enlisted the help of members of local Army and RAF units to mount a gala day featuring displays of weapons and a comprehensive programme of sports events at Dounby Showyard, where a savings centre would also be set up. The east Mainland was not left out and the agricultural sub-committee was meeting in the first days of August to organise a similar gala.

Competition between localities was a key aspect of the savings campaigns and, while the target of the week had been set at £100,000 with the committee recognising that this was a substantial amount of money, it was hoped that Orkney might be able to top the sum of £250,000 that had been raised by Caithness, which had also set a target of £100,000. The committee believed that Orkney could top this total, but only if every man, woman and child made the utmost effort to support the campaign.

The meeting of the committee held at the end of the month was chaired by Provost Flett and was mainly concerned with finalising the draft programme of events. Representatives from the forces and the police were also present to lend their support. It was fortunate that Chief Constable W. Colin Campbell was present as he had recently returned from a period of leave in his native Bridge of Allan. This had coincided with the local War Weapons Week campaign and so the Chief Constable was able to furnish various details and ideas of the events that had been organized to raise funds there. The committee also heard that local banks and post offices had agreed to extend their opening hours during the campaign to enable more people to purchase certificates.

We have already seen how the Kirkwall Naval Base Entertainments Committee had raised funds for charities and provided entertainment for servicemen and locals (most notably when they continued an amateur dramatics production during a substantial air raid in 1940). The group continued this fine tradition throughout 1941 and at the end of July it was recorded that from May the committee had donated £200 to various charities. The primary sources of this income were another Kirkwall Amateur Dramatics Society production ('Cuckoo in the Nest') in May and the ship's company concert ('The Pyramids') held at the beginning of July.

Donations from 'Cuckoo in the Nest' Production

Charity			
Balfour Hospital	£25		
Kirkwall & District Nursing Association	£15		
Toc-H, Kirkwall	£10		
Shipwrecked Fishermen & Mariners' Society	£10		
RNLI	£10		
Royal Naval Benevolent Trust	£20		
Royal Naval & Marine Orphan Home	£10		
Charitable Fund of Naval Officer-in-Charge, Kirkwall	£22	4s	6d
Total	**£122**	**4s**	**6d**

Donations from 'The Pyramids'

Charity			
Balfour Hospital	£15		
Shipwrecked Fishermen & Mariners' Society	£15		
Royal Naval Benevolent Trust	£20		
Royal Naval & Marine Orphan Home	£9	7s	10d
Charitable Fund of Naval Officer-in-Charge, Kirkwall	£10		
Total	**£69**	**7s**	**10d**
Total from Both Productions	**£191**	**12s**	**4d**

Companies were keen to demonstrate their patriotism by publicising their own contributions to war savings campaigns, and the Orkney War Weapons Week received a boost at the beginning of August when the Prudential Assurance Co. Ltd., which had two local branches at Kirkwall and one at Stromness, placed notices in the local press stating that it had already donated £5,000 to the campaign and none-too-subtly urging other Orcadians to follow the company's example by throwing their weight behind the campaign. Below the notice was a form which could be cut out and posted to the Prudential asking for details of their 3 per cent Savings Bond Policy. Aberdeen Savings Bank also placed adverts in the press urging people to support the war effort by placing their savings in a trustee savings bank.

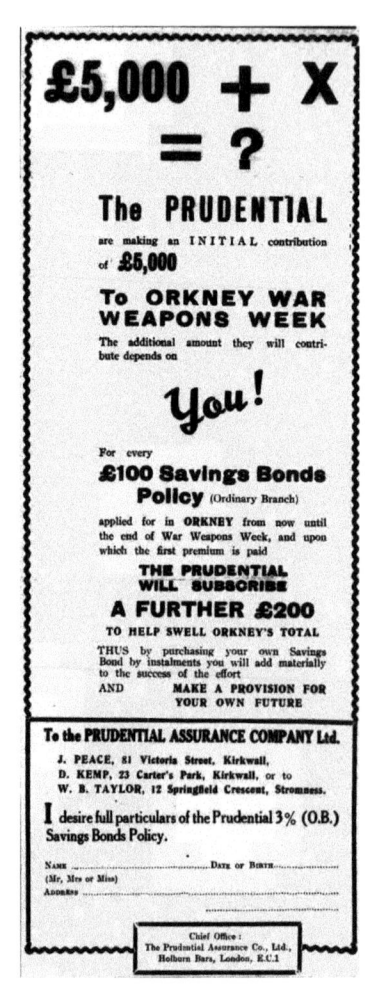

*Prudential Notice of Support for War Weapons Week (*Orkney Herald*)*

*Advert from Aberdeen Savings Bank for War Weapons Week (*Orkney Herald*)*

With just days to go before the beginning of the campaign, the Orkney committee was handed a slogan to go along with it provided, inadvertently, by Minister for Aircraft Production, Lieutenant Colonel Moore-Brabazon. He said 'Pound, pound, pound the enemy with Pounds, Pounds, Pounds of Savings'.[28] The slogan was speedily adopted as a means to motivate people to contribute all they could. They urged all to search and empty mantelpiece canisters, wallets, stockings, mattresses and other hiding places of money for the campaign.

One committee member, Mr Alex Calder, went even further stating that a significant number of people kept large amounts of money in such hiding places and, calling these folk 'delinquents, whose actions hinder the war effort', urged all such Orcadians to forgo these ways and keep on hand only what they required and to invest the rest in support of the war effort. In a further effort at encouragement he offered reassurance to thrifty Orcadians that money invested into the trustee savings bank could be withdrawn on demand at very short notice.

With the opening military parade being widely advertised, the local press even stoked enthusiasm by hinting that the salute would be taken 'by an important official whose name it is impossible, for reasons of security, to announce in advance'. The Kirkwall Grammar School Savings Group were also making their own contributions. Despite the children being on holiday, the honorary secretary of the group, Mr Gow, was on hand at the school four nights of the week to take donations. Mr Gow had also gathered a band of volunteers who had agreed to take on the burden of distributing leaflets and posters during the course of the week.

Kirkwall had arranged a considerably varied programme of events. One of those which was expected to prove extremely popular was the fancy dress parade on the evening of Tuesday, 19 August. Open to 'children of all ages from 6 to 60', it was hoped that a large turnout would ensue. A band from one of the services was to lead the parade from West Castle Street at 6.30pm when the judging would take place and prizes awarded to the best-dressed children.

Another item which was expected to be popular was the parade made up of the ARP and Civil Defence Services, due to take place on 21 August. This was to be accompanied by members of the Boy Scouts, Boys' Brigade and Girl Guides – although their numbers were somewhat depleted due to wartime conditions – and was organized by the Chief Warden and Sheriff-Clerk, Mr John White. The members of the three youth organizations named above were being urged to volunteer for the parade by Mr White so as to boost numbers. This was to be followed the next day by a fire-fighting display given by the men of the AFS. The full programme at Kirkwall is given below.

Kirkwall Programme of Events for War Weapons Week, 16-23 August 1941

Saturday 16 August

Opening address, march past of forces parade led by band, Market Green, 3pm

Banks open for War Weapons Week business only, 6-7pm

Service pipe band, mounting of the guard and address by Rev. Alexander, 7pm

Monday 18 August

Address by J. Storer Clouston & Mr Alexander Calder, Auction Mart, 11.30am

Display of war weapons, relics and trophies, Brandyquoy Park, 3-7pm. Admission 1s

.22 Shooting competition, Rifle Range, Willow Road, 6pm. Entry fee and prizes

Retreat Set by service pipe band, address by Mr H.O. Horne, mounting of guard, 7pm

Tuesday 19 August

Display of war weapons, relics and trophies, Brandyquoy Park, service band, 3-7pm. Admission 1s

.22 Shooting competition, Rifle Range, Willow Road, 6pm. Entry fee and prizes

Service band, fancy dress parade, West Castle Street (and through town), 6:30pm onwards

Wednesday 20 August

Inter-services and civilian sports, Bignold Park, 2pm

Band of the Royal Artillery, address by senior military officer, Market Green, 8pm

Thursday 21 August

Service pipe band, address by P.N. Sutherland Graeme, march past of civilian services, community singing led by RAF band, Market Green, 7pm

Friday 22 August

Service band, Market Green (Town Hall if wet), 3pm

Service band, display by Kirkwall Fire Brigade and AFS, address by Major Linklater, 7pm

Saturday 23 August

Service band, Market Green (Town Hall if wet), 3pm

Closing address by Provost Flett, announcement of sum, Retreat Set by service band, 8pm

Other Events

Ships which were in the vicinity during 16-18 would be open to public

Short films shown at local cinemas throughout the week

At Dounby the finishing touches were being put to the gala by the West Mainland Agricultural Society with a full programme of events, sports and displays. The three Stromness banks (the Commercial, the National and the Union) had agreed to have representatives in attendance at the show yard with facilities for investors.

The fancy dress parade, which took place on the evening of Tuesday, 19 August, was well attended and the large number of entrants, mainly children, made for a colourful spectacle. Led by a Royal Marines band, the parade attracted a good crowd and there were many laughs over the variety of costumes, some of which showed a keen observation of recent events. Prize winners were: 1st place – Muriel Isbister ('The Cracker'); 2nd place – Isobel Cheyne ('Buy Bombs for Berlin' – a cycle with a large cardboard bomb on it with various slogans); 3rd place – Maurice Manson (a German soldier); 4th place – Michael Stevens (Sacks). During the day aircraft from a nearby aerodrome flew low over the town dropping War Weapons Week pamphlets and the same 'raid' was carried out again two days later.

The sporting events held at Bignold Park on the following day also attracted large crowds. The entries were mainly from the forces and the competitions were keenly contested. One of the most popular events was the land-boat race between the three services. That evening, a Royal Artillery band played in Broad Street and an address was made on the Market Green by Major General Kemp MC. Using the story of the Three Little Pigs, General Kemp said that in the years before the war the country had built a house of straw, the year before the war, when crisis was close, they had built a house of wood which was a little more sturdy, but now they were having to build a house of bricks but, to do so they, would need to have the labour in place to build that house. In other words, according to the general, the country was involved in a total war but that some people did not realise this. He went on to say that if everyone recognised this reality then there would be no need for funds such as the War Weapons Week as all savings would have already been loaned to the country. He was at pains to point out that the savings effort must not stop once the week-long event had ended, but must continue without the specific savings campaigns.

The undoubted highlight of Thursday's events was the parade mounted by the members of the ARP and Civil Defence organizations, accompanied by the police, ATC, Boys' Brigade, and Girl Guides. The full extent of the ARP services was revealed to many Orcadians as contingents from the services were joined by representatives of the Fire Brigade, AFS, ambulances, rest service staff, demolition squads, decontamination squads, and air raid wardens. The parade was led by a pipe band from a

1941: A LOSING BATTLE   65

Top   Sinclair Bill   R   ?   John   Jackie David   David
         Ross   Moss Kemp Kelday Tulloch Miller Eunson Moss
Middle Jim John Joe   Ian   Norman Ernie   John   Allie   Jim William   David
Work Muir Walker McGillivary Cooper Hourston Dearness Seatter Scott Donaldson Logie
       Bottom Norman Charles Bob   John   Robert Ronald   ?
              Peace Findlater Firth Goodall Wilson Cheyne -----

Kirkwall ATC, pictured in 1940. (Sylvia Walker)

Highland regiment and afterwards there was a session of communal singing led by an RAF band.

Of the many addresses which were delivered during the War Weapons Week, the most intriguing was probably that by Mr P.N. Sutherland Graeme of Graemeshall, Holm, at the Market Green following the parade of civilian services. In his address Mr Graeme firstly praised Orcadians for the contributions they had made to the war effort so far, highlighting the two fighters which had been paid for and the substantial sum of money raised for war savings along with the current, ongoing, efforts for War Weapons Week. He then revealed that the aim of £100,000 had been 'smashed to smithereens within twenty-four hours' and that the indicator of funds raised currently stood at over £200,000 and he would not be surprised if the final sum topped £300,000. Mr Graeme then went on to say that Orkney had not been content to raise just the £100,000 that would buy five bombers, or ten tanks, or twenty fighters, or thirty anti-aircraft guns. Nor was Orkney content to settle for the £200,000 at which the current figure stood, but that by raising £300,000 Orkney would be able to provide one of the new corvettes which were now being used in the Battle of the Atlantic.

He then went on to exhort Orcadians to even further efforts, telling them that it was not just their duty but their privilege to raise these funds at a time when they, as a country, were fighting for the things in which they believed and that one true test of patriotism was financial sacrifice which demonstrated the will to win. Orcadians, he told them, could be proud of their commitment to the war effort. He then relayed how he had often been told by servicemen who had served in Orkney of how welcome they had been made to feel on the islands, renowned for their hospitality, before reminding them that the first duty of a host was to ensure guests had everything they needed.

Standing upon an air raid shelter, he enlarged on the theme of hospitality. Mr Graeme told his listeners that as Orkney was once more host to a mighty fleet, as it had been during the First World War, it behoved the inhabitants to make sure that they provided all that was needed for the service personnel of Britain who were fighting this war. Moving on to what they were fighting for, Mr Graeme said that this time they were fighting not only for their lives, but for a positive and lasting peace. The sword, he said, should immediately be converted to the ploughshare of peace once the war was won and told listeners that the arts of peace must be allowed and encouraged to flourish along with the genius of man being rededicated to the benefit of mankind. Mr Graeme became quite passionate in his address on the need for lasting peace saying 'We want to see the end of this fearsome object upon which I stand. We want to hear the last of the sirens … Let God's creatures live their lives as God intended them to live. The creator meant the air for the birds, beneath the sea for the fishes. For heaven's sake, let's return both to their legitimate owners.' He then went on to say that people wanted 'an end to want and depression. But we have to fight for this. We have to fight to win peace, and we have got to deserve peace.'[29] Concluding his lengthy speech, Mr Graeme told listeners to renew their commitment to the effort and to go immediately to the place where investments could be made.

Throughout the week the local cinemas were showing short films which encouraged people to invest. The showings at the Albert Kinema were especially popular and, on Thursday, the audience was addressed by Councillor Charles Archibald. The address was a rather lengthy one but the nub of the speech was that the councillor wanted people to think of their investments not as money but as ships, guns, bombs, planes and explosives and 'as something to raise a protective wall of fire round our much-loved islands ... so shall this wall of fire with which your money has helped to surround us be of such an all-consuming and all-destroying fire to our enemies that their blitzkrieg fire will appear in comparison as that of a damp squib that has fizzled out'.[30]

Another interesting address was given the next day by Major Eric Linklater of Merkister, Dounby. Major Linklater was a famous writer who had been a Territorial officer in the Black Watch during the First World War, being wounded before becoming a sniper, and also serving with the Orkney Fortress Company of the Royal Engineers. In the current war he had founded a weekly newspaper for service personnel in January 1940 entitled *The Orkney Blast* and had recently returned from a tour of Faroe and Iceland which had culminated in the publication of his pamphlet, *The Northern Garrisons*.

Major Linklater began his address in humorous fashion by jokingly declaiming the sabotage of the public address system by an unknown fifth-columnist and joked that this meant he had to shout and would probably wake up with laryngitis. His speech continued in a similar vein as he told the audience that his presence there served no purpose as he was only going to tell them to do what they had already done or had determined to do.

That, of course, was to donate every possible penny to enable the government and the forces to bring the war to a successful conclusion as soon as possible. He claimed that there were three main reasons for acting in this way. The first was that they were not being asked to give money, but to invest it for a good cause and at a fair rate of interest. Major Linklater, however, continued in a humorous manner telling the audience that, so unscrupulous were governments, that if they did not invest then the government would probably just take the money off them and not at 3 per cent interest.

The second reason Major Linklater gave was that 'nowadays there is practically nothing you can do with your money anyhow'. He then continued by humorously referring to the shortages of cigarettes, alcohol, clothing and petrol meaning that with the spare change he had there was nothing to do with it but to invest in war bonds. The third reason, which was, according to Major Linklater, the most important, was to end the war as quickly as possible but only on the terms that the people of Britain wanted: total victory. To achieve this the fighting had to go on and had to be paid for.

The gala sports day that took place at Dounby Show Park on Saturday afternoon attracted a huge crowd with the sporting events being closely contested by both servicemen and civilians. The takings for the event amounted to £115 14s and a side-collection which was taken was donated to the Red Cross.

Small, locally organized, events took place throughout the week to raise funds for the

Major Eric Linklater. (The Tatler)

campaign. A concert and dance, for example, brought in £21 2s 6d while the opening of the grounds of Balfour Castle raised £72 3s 6d and Captain Denison of the *Iona*, which ferried people to and from the castle, donated £30 10s. As a further incentive for visitors a 15s war savings certificate was offered as a prize to anyone who guessed the amount of money that would be raised during the event. Miss R. Garrioch of 10 Clay Loan, Kirkwall was the lucky winner with her estimate of £73 1s 6d being the closest.

All of the communities across Orkney were involved in the campaign and some even found a way to make further donations over and above those investments for the War Weapons Week. At Shapinsay £123 16s was raised through a variety of functions which were held through the week. This money was in addition to that which was invested as part of the War Weapons Week and was instead handed over directly to the Exchequer.

Following the end of the campaign, Mr Graeme of Graemeshall opened up the beautiful gardens of his home for a small charge which was used to defray the costs of the War Weapons Week. The house attracted a constant stream of people and a number of interesting relics of Graemehouse in the past and during the First World War were available to view, while one of Mr Graeme's granddaughters, Lady Elspeth Walthaw, had a busy afternoon taking children for rides on her Shetland pony.

Four days after the close of the campaign several of the leading original members of the committee (Lord Lieutenant A. Baikie of Tankerness, Mr J. Storer Clouston, Provost P.C. Flett of Kirkwall, Provost J. Marwick of Stromness and Mr A. Calder of Sebay) placed a letter in the local press thanking the people of Orkney. They were, they stated, proud of the efforts of the people of Orkney in smashing the original aim of the fund despite the other calls on their funds during the war. In fact, Orkney had almost quadrupled the original intended sum and the total raised stood at £393,888 7s 4d and it was believed that when the final tally was made this would rise to more than

£400,000. The sum so far reached was worked out as an average investment of over £16 per head of population.

Progress of Orkney War Weapons Week

Day	TOTALS		
Monday, 18 August			
3.30pm	£65,000		
7.30pm	£86,000		
Tuesday, 19 August			
11am	£99,000		
3.30pm	£104,771	15s	
7.30pm	£115,393		
Wednesday, 20 August			
11am	£118,000		
3.30pm	£128,760		
7.30pm	£150,973	6s	1d
Thursday, 21 August			
11am	£166,184	19s	7d
8pm	£182,000		
Friday, 22 August			
10.15am	£201,705	1s	7d
3pm	£209,038	16s	7d
6pm	£225,029	18s	6d
Saturday, 23 August			
10.15am	£302,313	13s	6d
2pm	£332,225	11s	
7.50pm	£358,034	19s	
Tuesday, 26 August			
2.30pm	£393,888	7s	4d

Despite the determination to contribute to the war effort there were still cases of people avoiding new regulations appearing before the courts on Orkney. On 19 August, while the War Weapons Week was in full swing, three such cases, all of them linked, were heard by Sheriff Brown at Kirkwall. Mr John George Stanger had allegedly fallen foul of the Livestock (Restriction on Slaughtering) Order 1940, being accused by two of his employees of having caused a pig to be slaughtered without possessing a licence from the Ministry of Food. Mr James Flett, representing Mr Stanger, told the court that Mr Stanger pleaded guilty to the charge but that he had merely followed his practice of fifty years and he had no idea that he had done wrong.

Ignorance of the law, of course, is no defence and the Fiscal replied that he could not believe an experienced farmer such as Mr Stanger, who farmed on a fairly large scale, could be unaware of the regulations which had been in force for some time now and that if this was allowed to pass then other farmers would use it to get around rationing regulations. Mr Flett once again stated that his client had acted only in accordance with long-established tradition on his farm, that he was unaware of the regulation and pleaded with the court to show leniency for what was a first offence. Sheriff Brown was not moved by this argument and stated that he could not accept Mr Stanger was ignorant of the law regarding the slaughtering of livestock for human consumption. He therefore imposed a fine of £5 upon Mr Stanger with the alternative of thirty days imprisonment.

The second part of the case involved a Dounby merchant, Mr James Oag, who was charged with being in possession of the carcass of the above pig without a licence. It was illegal for anyone without a licence to have in their possession, sell, expose for sale or otherwise dispose of such a carcass. Solicitor, Mr William Davis, stated that his client knew nothing of the order in question and that this was a mere technical breach of the order and that the accused had no profit from having the carcass in his possession. He therefore suggested that a suitable punishment would be a simple admonishment. The Sheriff said he would defer sentencing until he had heard the final part of the case.

The final part of the story of the pig that did not go to market involved another merchant. John George Jolly of Harray was accused of producing 134lbs of bacon from a carcass without possession of the necessary licence contrary to the Bacon (Licensing of Producers) Order, 1939. Representing Mr Jolly, Mr C.E.S. Wallis tendered a guilty plea. The Fiscal told Sheriff Brown that Ministry of Food employees had entered a shed on Mr Jolly's premises and found five pieces of pork in the course of being turned into bacon. Four of these were traced back to the pig mentioned above and it was noted that Mr Jolly's initial claim that he had bought the meat ordinarily and was preparing to pickle and preserve it was proven false by the lack of string marks on the bacon. Mr Jolly, the Sheriff was told, did not have a licence to produce bacon, to which Mr Wallis stated that his client was a licensed dealer in meat and that he had only agreed to cure the pork which had been brought to him by Mr Oag so as to prevent it going bad. Mr Jolly also stated that, in his opinion, it would have been better to sell the carcass as fresh pork.

Sheriff Brown sentenced both Mr Oag and Mr Jolly to pay £5 or face thirty days' imprisonment and in summing up the case said that he believed it represented a scheme to avoid the rationing regulation and was thus a very serious matter. He added that any further such cases brought before him would be more harshly punished. Indeed, Sheriff Brown had been lenient as the possible punishment for such offences included a fine of up to £100, three months imprisonment, or both.

CHAPTER 4

1942: Struggling on

While the bulk of Orcadians had made the most of the somewhat muted Hogmanay celebrations, it was clear that, for the majority, the war, and particularly the reverses suffered during 1941, were foremost in their minds, along with a mingled sense of trepidation and a determination to see the war through to a winning conclusion.

For the Rev. David Bell of the Paterson Church, Kirkwall, however, it was a lack of piety and the fear that people were missing out on the inspiring messages he sought to spread which seems to have been the main issue over the New Year period. Mr Bell wrote an extensive column for the *Orkney Herald* under the headline 'Kirkwall Minister Ridicules Flimsy Excuses. Inspiring New Year Call'. Mr Bell stated that he had heard all sorts of excuses for a failure to attend church services with the most common being that the services were too long. This, he asserted, was a preferable way of spending two hours rather than in a picture house. Another excuse he had noted included the fact that a service taking place after 6pm could not be attended due to the blackout, while attendances at dances and other social functions held in the hours of darkness did not seem to have been affected in the slightest. Yet another was the weather. A wet, windy and cold day deterred many from going to church, but did not deter Orcadians from going about their other business, added this somewhat pompous man.

These complaints formed part of the sermon given by Mr Bell on Sunday, 4 January and, apparently because there had been few to hear it, he then went on to recreate the majority of it in his article, taking up three columns of newsprint! The bulk of his extremely long-winded sermon used the Exodus of the Israelites from Egypt as its basis, the main thrust being that people would do well to remember the lessons in the tale as it was instructive for the present in that people should put the events of the early years of the war behind them, be proud of the wounds and hardships suffered, and move forward.

The second part of Mr Bell's sermon focused on a criticism of his colleagues, many of whom, according to the Rev. Bell, had given in to a spirit of defeatism as a result of the slackening attendances amongst their congregations. Explaining the attitude of some colleagues, he said that they 'sit down and wring their hands, and say, "We do well if we but keep the church doors open, if we hold on, until the coming of a better day".' Mr Bell argued that this was a poor attitude and urged his colleagues that simply keeping the doors open was not enough, instead it was for them to 'storm the citadels of evil, to rouse the people from their lethargy' and to point out to them that only through faith in Christ could peace and freedom be won. He then went on to enjoin his colleagues to hear 'the clear call being sounded today, to clean up our own lives, to overhaul our Church life, to win again to a burning ardour ... those who have grown cold in their worship and lax in their service'. Once again, Mr Bell placed the blame upon his colleagues saying that there were many young men who were attracted to Christ but not to the Church because they viewed the priesthood as slack and unenthusiastic.

Concluding his marathon written sermon the Rev. Bell said, 'I believe that I speak in the name of God when I say there can be no talk of peace today – that the call is rather to a greater effort, a grander sacrifice' and, after the war was won and the evil they faced vanquished, that a long-lasting peace and brotherhood be established. Bell finished by saying that this message of going forward for a great good applied especially to those 'as individuals, as men and women, who have taken their place in the ranks of Christ's army, as people who must continue to endure all the agonising of the greatest war the world has ever known'.[31]

Quite what the majority of people on Orkney made of the sermon is hard to judge. There were many people of strong faith on the island, but the hectoring and rather arrogant tone of Mr Bell's haranguing sermon must surely have also further alienated some, especially those who were well aware of the sacrifices being made and which had already been made by the people of Orkney. As for his colleagues' reactions, once again, it is hard to imagine that they would appreciate this sermon, casting doubts on their own strength of faith and ability to inspire as it did.

Others within the Church were performing rather more mundane but valuable services. The St Magnus Canteen, run under the auspice of the Church of Scotland Huts' Committee, had proved a great success in its aim of providing food, drink, shelter and recreation for the thousands of service personnel who were stationed on or passed through Orkney. On 2 January the superintendents of the canteen, the Rev. David Crosbie and his wife, entertained the volunteer women staff of the canteen to an afternoon tea in the staff quarters. The Reverend and his wife had been in charge for four months and had done their utmost to ensure that working at the canteen was an enjoyable experience for the volunteers and this effort was rewarded as the volunteers presented him and his wife with a travelling rug and a copy of *The Orkneyinga Saga* in appreciation of the 'happy fellowship they had enjoyed under the leadership of the superintendents'.[32] The tea was also a farewell as the Rev. Crosbie and his wife were due to depart the following week for a similar post in Edinburgh. This meant that the couple would not be on hand to witness the opening of the newly constructed extension to the canteen, which the volunteers were shown around, as it would not open until the end of January.

Hogmanay also brought a New Year message from the Food Controller for the north-east of Scotland. In the message he admitted that 1941 had seen control orders extended to a variety of foodstuffs and that in some places this had caused short-term difficulties and shortages but that, in the main, people had accepted these measures with good cheer. There had, he admitted, been some grousing amongst those who still did not appreciate that the aim of rationing and food control was to ensure fair shares for all people, but that there had been little of this in the north-east and particularly on Orkney. He concluded his message by thanking the people, the wholesalers and shopkeepers, and reminding all of them to especially remember the sacrifices being made by the men of the Merchant Navy in bringing food to Britain. Such an exhortation was probably unnecessary to the people of Orkney, who had so many relatives and friends serving in this force.

Despite the islands entering their fourth year of war the mundane duties of justice continued in the first week of 1942. The massive numbers of service personnel who had been posted to the islands largely got on well with the Orcadians, but the increased population did cause some problems. One of these was an increase in the number of motor-vehicle accidents on previously quiet roads. On 6 January a case came before the Sheriff's Court at Kirkwall demonstrating this phenomenon. Driver Charles William Turner, Royal Army Service Corps (RASC), was charged with, on 29 November 1941, having driven an Army vehicle recklessly, so that it collided with a privately-owned Ford Model 8 car driven by a local joiner, James William Louttit of Woodstock, Holm. His passenger, Mrs Mary Winifred Brown, the wife of a local schoolteacher from East Holm, sustained head injuries which resulted in her having to spend three weeks in bed. There was also an alternative, and lesser, charge of careless driving made against the defendant. Driver Turner was defended by a second lieutenant from his unit and in view of the contradictory evidence and lack of witnesses the case was found not proven.

Many RAF airmen lost their lives while training through accidents or as a result of mechanical failures. Amongst them was Sergeant Albert David Matthews (22). Sergeant Matthews was an air gunner based at RAF Newmarket with 3 Group Training Flight when, on 6 January, he was detailed to take part in a gunnery practice operation aboard Wellington IC (L7863). As the Wellington took off one of the engines caught fire and the pilot, Flight Sergeant F.T. Miniken attempted to make a forced landing but the aircraft struck an embankment and then a building and eight of the ten crewmen aboard were killed.[33] Sergeant Matthews was a married man and left a young widow, Mary Elizabeth Matthews, at her home on St Ola. His widow had the following inscription placed upon the young airman's headstone: 'UNSEEN BY THE WORLD HE STANDS BY MY SIDE AND WHISPERS, DEAR ONE DEATH CANNOT DIVIDE'.

Orkney suffered two more civilian losses due to enemy action during an attack on Shetland on 21 January. The pattern of small-scale hit-and-run raids on both Orkney and Shetland (as well as other parts of north-eastern Scotland) had continued over the winter months and on this day two Orcadian women who were living at the South Lighthouse, Fair Isle, were killed. Mother and daughter Margaret Helen Smith (50) and Margaret 'Gretta' Smith (10) were the wife and daughter of lighthouseman Mr William Smith. Margaret Helen Smith (née Groat) was the daughter of Mr and Mrs Isaac Groat of Hools, Widewall, South Ronaldsay. Gretta had recently made the news when, shortly after the family had arrived at Shetland, she had suffered acute appendicitis and had had to be ferried to hospital through 90 miles of stormy seas by the Lerwick lifeboat. The Smiths also had a young son, Norman, who was at school at Hope Higher Grade School, St Margaret's Hope. Until recently the Smith family had been living at John O'Groats where they had been very popular in the local community.

The next savings campaign, Warships Week, had been due to take place on Orkney during June but a meeting of the Warships

Week committee held in February heard and agreed to a request from the Scottish Savings Committee to bring the date of the campaign forward to the last week in May. The request was due to a further request from the Exchequer which asked for all Warships Week campaigns to have been completed by the end of March, with an extension for Scotland until the end of May. The selection of the Warship Week Executive Committee demonstrated the success of the previous campaign as it was compiled of the same people that had taken part in the War Weapons campaign.

Even when the week-long campaigns were not being run, the savings campaign went on with local groups, fostered by a sense of competition and sense of regional pride, keenly encouraging their members to invest the most they possibly could. From early November 1941 to mid-February 1942 savings groups on Orkney had invested the total of £8,234 12s 5d, with the churches of Kirkwall setting a particularly fine example. The St Magnus Savings Group had thus far saved well over £22,000, the Paterson Church Group had reached almost £14,000 while the Kirkwall Women's Unionist Association had saved over £6,500. This latter organization had recently been featured on a BBC broadcast on 7 February. The association had set their target for this round of saving with the intent of purchasing an ambulance.

Orkney Savings Groups, November 1941-February 1942

Group			
St Magnus Cathedral	£22,277	8s	9d
Alfred Mackay	£10,976	18s	2d
Paterson Church	£13,911	9s	8d
Kirkwall Women's Unionist Association	£6,517	18s	2d
Kirkwall Grammar School	£5,453	7s	6d
Orkney County Council, Roads Dept.	£5,176	9s	11d

Stronsay Church	£5,076	15s	5d
RAF Bignold Park	£3,132	16s	6d
Rendall Church	£2,314	6s	6d
St Ola WRI	£1,551	15s	
R. Garden Ltd.	£1,274	17s	3d
Kirkwall Shipping	£840	9s	11d
Glaitness Laundry	£817	9s	6d
James Flett & Sons	£784	10s	6d
J&W Tait	£776	8s	3d
George Bain	£765		6d
Orkney County Police	£625	12s	10d
Rousay, Egilshay & Wyre Co-operative	£483	16s	6d
Highland Park	£274	4s	5d
Scapa School	£256	12s	6d
Deerness WRI	£228		
Mackay & Wallace	£97	11s	3d
Evie School	£31	2s	6d
Total	£83,645	1s	7d

Lessons had clearly been learned from the past savings campaigns and it seems that enthusiasm on Orkney was undimmed. Not only were the preparations for Warships Week in full swing but the committee was even making plans for the campaign in 1943 which would be in support of the RAF and entitled Wings for Victory Week. The target fot the week had already been set and it was hoped that Orkney would raise sufficient money to fund the purchase of seven Catalina flying boats. In order to stoke early interest in the scheme the local press were informed that if the islands successfully reached their target they would receive the flying log books of the seven aircraft after the war as a reward. It would seem that the Wings for Victory campaign was receiving widespread support even at this stage as committees had already been formed to choose parish targets, organise events and launch district campaigns at Birsay, Eday, Evie, Harray, Orphir, Sandwick and Shapinsay.

Major Eric Linklater continued his fervent defence of and appreciation for the Army in a short article in the *Orkney Herald*. Major Linklater related how he had recently heard that one or two people were referring to the Army as being the Cinderella service. He admitted that it had done a few dirty jobs in recent years, but informed readers that in his recent tours of various garrisons he had been impressed by the patient yet determined attitude of the soldiers he had encountered. Furthermore, they had been doing their best to make the most of their solitary and sometimes boring posts by taking full advantage of the excellent and broad educational scheme which had been supported by the Army.

The construction work on the Orkney barriers continued apace with the workforce engaged on the project now totalling approximately 2,000 men. The contractors had received a boost to their efforts to secure labour following the defeat of the Italians in the North African Campaign and by the early months of 1942 large numbers of these Italian PoWs were being housed in Britain, with over 1,300 being sent to Orkney to work on the defences. The government had to find a way to justify this as the Geneva Convention forbade the use of PoWs as labour on wartime construction efforts, and so the barriers were therefore re-classified as improvements to the communications on Orkney. To house these prisoners, three camps were set up on the islands: two on Burray, for 700 prisoners, and one on Lamb Holm housing some 600 Italian prisoners.

The Italian PoWs left behind several mementoes of their enforced visit to the Isles. The most famous of these is the Italian Chapel, which was built at Lamb. The camp priest at Camp 60, Father Giacobazzi, had a request for two Nissen huts to be joined together to be used as a chapel and a resident of the camp, Domenico Chiocchetti, an artist, was placed in charge of the decoration of the chapel. In his work he was assisted by two other inmates, Guisseppe Palumbi, who was a blacksmith, and a cement worker named Domenico Buttapasta.

The Italian Chapel. (CC3.0, Vidarlo)

Originally, permission had only been given for a painting above the altar but, realising how talented Chiocchetti was, the camp commandant gave his permission for the work to continue until the entire chapel was decorated. This proved a wise decision as, not only was it popular with the inmates, but it has now gone on to become one of Orkney's foremost tourist attractions.

As the brutal Italian campaign continued, the three squadrons of B-24 Liberator bombers based in the theatre found themselves being increasingly used in a tactical bombing campaign against Romania. On the night of 6 / 7 May a mixed force consisting of Wellingtons and Liberators was dispatched to bomb industrial sites, railway bridges and marshalling yards in the Romanian capital, Bucharest. Five of the bombers failed to return. Amongst them was Liberator VI (EV841, H) of 178 Squadron. The bomber had taken off from Foggia shortly after 9pm detailed to attack marshalling yards, but was shot down by a night-fighter and crashed at Belciug killing five of the seven men aboard. One of the air gunners on board the Liberator was Orcadian airman Flight Sergeant James Robert Velzian (19), the son of William and Betsy Velzian from Kirbuster.[34]

Italian PoWs Outside the Chapel. (Unknown)

We have already seen that many an Orcadian man fell victim while serving in the Merchant Navy. On 2 May yet another was lost. Second Radio Officer John Alexander Paris Campbell (22) was from Cromwell Road, Kirkwall and was the eldest of two sons. When the war began John had been training in Edinburgh as a teacher in technical subjects and had previously spent two years in college on shore before going to sea as a radio operator. He had been serving since the early months of the war and had been commended for his coolness under fire after his ship came under repeated attack. On the day of his death John was one of the 56-strong crew of the SS *Cape Corso* (Glasgow) sailing as part of the Russia-bound Convoy PQ-15 when the ship was attacked by torpedo-equipped Heinkel He 111 aircraft. Hit by a torpedo, the merchant ship sank quickly and only six of the crew survived.[35]

With the success of the previous year's savings campaign it was with high expectations that Orkney prepared for its Warships

The SS Cape Corso, *lost on a Russia Convoy. (Unknown)*

Week, scheduled to run from 23-30 May. As had happened previously, the trustee savings banks and the post office threw their weight behind the campaign and agreed to extend their opening hours during the week to allow more people to invest. The aim for the week was to raise the sum of £120,000 in order to adopt the corvette HMS *Ness*. Under slogans such as 'Lend Freely for Freedom' the people of Orkney were once again urged to give everything they could afford.

Although most events at this time were geared towards the Warships Week, there were other events taking place. With Britain involved in a total war it was vital that women ensured that they were doing their utmost to contribute to the war effort. Indeed, many young women were increasingly viewing the war as opening up new opportunities to them, ones which otherwise would have remained closed. This especially applied to some of the young women on Orkney, many of whom had not much experience beyond their own small communities.

Three days before the start of the campaign the Holm WRI were treated to a talk from a Ministry of Information lecturer named Mrs Gardner. The speaker needed no introduction as she was a native of the parish and had taught at the West School. Addressing her subject of 'Women's Activities in Wartime' Mrs Gardner gave an interesting insight into the work of the ATS, NAAFI, Nursing Services, WAAFS, WFC, WLA, WRNS, and other canteen services. She was at pains to point out that, unlike what had always been the case during the early years of the war, the living conditions experienced by these young women were superb and that this could be further helped by housewives living in the areas where these women were stationed opening up their homes to them and making them feel part of the local community. Moving on from the services, Mrs Gardner expressed her belief that every woman should acquaint herself with basic first-aid techniques and that notice should be taken of the many pamphlets issued dealing with the war on the kitchen front. The lecture was very well received and the women present vowed to do their utmost. Following the lecture, a tea was served and flags were sold in aid of the Warships Week campaign.

While the War Weapons Week total had been shown on a large thermometer during the previous year, the Warships Week gauge was more in theme and consisted of a large cut-out of a sailor climbing a 36ft mast on the Market Green at Kirkwall. Once again, the campaign was opened with a military march parade and salute. The guest of honour on this occasion was Vice-Admiral L.V. Wells CB DSO, the flag officer commanding Orkney and Shetland. Also on the saluting platform was the Lord Lieutenant, Mr Baikie and the Director of the Women's Royal Naval Service (WRNS), Mrs Vera Laughton-Matthews, who carried the unofficial rank of rear admiral. They were joined by a strong naval contingent and representatives of the other services. Giving his address, Vice Admiral Wells said that with Orkney being the main naval base in both this war and the previous one, Orkney and its residents had a close bond with the service and went on to describe some of the activities in which the RN was engaged. Moving on, he expressed his expectation that the figure for which the community was aiming would be smashed and that the type of vessel they were hoping to adopt, a corvette, was the type of ship which the RN needed at this juncture to escort merchant convoys across the Atlantic, to Russia and elsewhere in far-flung theatres of war. Fully aware of the many Orcadians who were members of the Merchant Navy, he praised the courage of the men of this service. In conclusion, Vice-Admiral Wells quoted the words of a popular song of some years ago:

> *We don't want to fight, but by Jingo if we do,*
> *We've got the ships,*
> *We've got the men,*
> *We've got the money, too*

This song, he said, gave birth to the word 'jingoism' and, while acknowledging that jingoism could be a fault, he said that it was also true that the British had been 'too prone to belittle ourselves. No wonder foreigners thought we are decadent ... Today the Navy fights on every ocean. We've got the men – the finest seamen we have ever had. We want the ships – and we want YOUR money, too.' The speech was met with loud acclaim and applause.

Following the speech, the secretary of the Warships Week Committee, Mr John W. Dickson, read out a telegram from the First Lord of the Admiralty which expressed best wishes and encouragement for the Orkney campaign. The telegram told the people of Orkney that with the extension of the naval war into the Pacific theatre, the RN had never been more stretched and needed all of the matériel, men and money that it could get. Further telegrams were read from the Chancellor of the Exchequer and from Mr Henry W. Scarth of Breckness, the Deputy District Commissioner, who was unable to attend the opening ceremony.

Following the speeches, the parade began, with the Vice-Admiral taking the salute. It was led by sailors, Royal Marines and WRNS and was followed by representatives of the Army (including mechanised units), ATS, RAF airmen, WAAFs, ATC and Home Guard. The parade was accompanied by music provided by a pipe band from a Highland regiment. The Home

Members of an Orkney Home Guard Platoon. (I Hourston)

Guard contingent in the parade was particularly large with members from Kirkwall, East and West Mainland platoons present. By nightfall on 26 May the total stood at £94,000.

Although Sunday, 24 May was not officially a part of the campaign there were two RN ships in harbour at Orkney which were open to members of the public in aid of the Warships Week fund. On 25 May the main attraction was the display of weapons on Market Green, Kirkwall. The RN, FAA, Army and Home Guard worked together to produce what was described as a very instructive and comprehensive display. Personnel from all of the above services were available to give demonstrations and to explain matters to interested members of the public. The weapons displayed included: a naval torpedo, various mines, mortars, field and anti-aircraft artillery, bren-gun carriers, predictors, sound locators and searchlights, rangefinders and a wide variety of personal arms. The Home Guard contingent were at particular pains to show how their own arsenal of effective weaponry was expanding. To demonstrate some of the working of the anti-aircraft technology, a simulated attack was launched by a friendly aircraft. The show proved hugely popular and was equally busy when it was repeated on 27 May.

During the Warships Week campaign the Secretary of State for Scotland, Mr Thomas Johnston, paid an unrelated flying visit to Orkney in order to assess the situation in the county and to get to know the local leaders. Arriving by air from Shetland on the Sunday, Mr Johnston enjoyed a pleasant visit as the meetings between himself and various leaders of the local authorities revealed no especial problems, a fact alluded to by Mr Johnston during his meeting with the members of Kirkwall Town Council. The main topics discussed concerned manpower and transport and although no large problems arose, Mr Johnston at least gained a working knowledge of the people who were in charge in Orkney and a sense of how the war was affecting the islands. During his visit Mr Johnston revealed that overall the health of the nation was very good and, for the first time in history, there was no reason for anyone in Scotland to go hungry but that it was a shame that it had taken a war to produce this state of affairs.

Donations, large and small, continued to pour in and in an effort to encourage further efforts, the local press placed the names of some of the donors within their pages every day of the campaign. On 25 May the *Orkney Herald* featured a list of ten donors.

List of Selected Donors on 25 May

Donor			
Scottish Union & National Insurance Co.	£5,000		
Eagle Star Insurance Co.	£2,500		
Collection at public inspection of RN ships on 24 May	£26	11s	3d
Deerness Home Guard Dance	£21	11s	
Master Hamish Bruce, collection at aquarium display	£2		4d
Mr James Hourston, Gerwin, Orphir	£1	17s	6d
Toronto Orkney & Shetland Society	£11	3s	6d
Ladies Section of Kirkwall Golf Club	£4		
Anonymous Donor, Longhope	£6		
RN -v- RAF Football Match, Sunday	£4	8s	8d

The combined ENSA and Kirkwall Amateur Dramatics Society production of 'Tonight at 8.30', which was shown at the Naval Cinema on Friday and Saturday evenings, proved to be a great success with reviewers describing it as being 100 per cent first rate entertainment, containing something to please everyone.

As in the previous year a wide programme of events was organized for the campaign week. On 27, 29 and 30 May the Temperance Hall in Kirkwall hosted what it advertised as the 'Show of Shows'. This had been organized by the commanding officer of the Orkney and Shetlands Entertainments Scheme. Prices for this show were set at 5s 6d and 3s 6d for reserved seats and 1s 6d for entry on the night (service personnel were admitted on the night for half price). The Orkney West Mainland Agricultural Society once again organized a Gala Day which was held at Dounby Park on the final day of the campaign at 2.30pm. Events included Highland dancing, races for fathers,

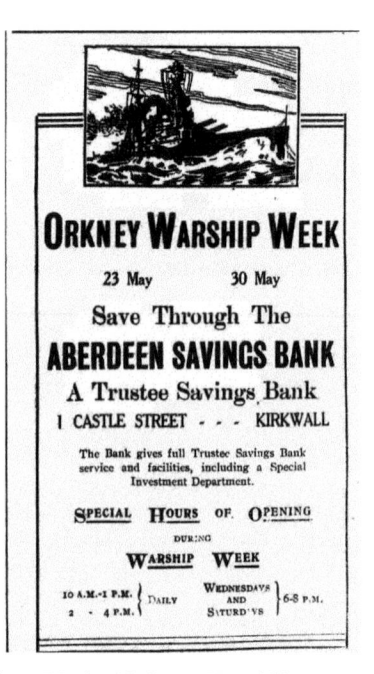

Selection of posters advertising Warships Week. (Orkney Herald)

mothers and children, tug-of-war, jumping, tossing the caber, putting the shot and track events. Entertainment was provided by a drum and pipe band from a Highland regiment and an RAF band. Prizes were available for many of the competitive events and entrance cost 1s for civilians and officers, and 6d for other ranks in uniform and children under the age of 14.

Second Half of Orkney's Warships Week Campaign

Wednesday, 27 May

Sports meeting, Balfour Mains Farm, Shapinsay, 2pm. Followed by dance in Drill Hall

Sports meeting, Bignold Park, Kirkwall, 3pm

Army display, physical training and dancing, Broad Street, Kirkwall, 7pm

Table tennis competition, Kirkwall Town Hall, 7.15pm

Ceremony of the Keys, Broad Street, Kirkwall, 8.10pm

Officers (all services) dance, Kirkwall Drill Hall, 9pm

Thursday, 28 May

War weapons display, Broad Street, Kirkwall, 3pm

Children's carnival parade, Kirkwall, 6.30pm

Dance (open), Kirkwall Drill Hall, 9pm. Tickets 15s (couple), 7s 6d (single)

Friday, 29 May

Table tennis, Kirkwall Town Hall, 7.15pm

ENSA & Kirkwall Dramatic Society show, Kirkwall Temperance Hall, 8.30pm

RN dance (RN and WRNS personnel), Kirkwall Drill Hall, 8pm

Dance (table tennis competitors and supporters), Kirkwall Town Hall, 9pm

Saturday, 30 May

Gala, Dounby (gate proceeds to Red Cross), 2.30pm

Football: Scottish Touring XI -v- The Army, Bignold Park, Kirkwall, 3pm

Royal Marines Band, Kirkwall, 3pm
Royal Marines Band, Market Green, Kirkwall, 6pm
Pipe music, Market Green, Kirkwall, 7pm
Announcement of final result, Market Green, Kirkwall, 7.30pm

Other Events

Soveran and Palace Road tennis court tournaments, Kirkwall (27-29 May)

Bowling tournaments, Kirkwall

Boxing tournaments, Kirkwall

A glance at the list of events above will show that sporting competitions were at the forefront of the fundraising efforts. Large crowds attended the table tennis tournament on the various nights and were treated to scintillating play by members of the Orkney League. On the first day of the tournament the winners were the Pioneers, with the Wanderers in second place after the victors defeated them 21-4. The prizes were awarded by Group Captain Grace, RAF. On Monday evening the highlight was the Ladies' Singles Championship, which was fought out in a best of three final between Wren Brown and Mrs Holt. A hard-fought match saw Wren Brown win the title, 21-13, 21-11, 21-13 in a 'best of five' round. The prizes on this night were awarded by the Director of the WRNS, Mrs Vera Laughton Matthews. The ladies' final was followed by an exhibition match between the captain of the Pioneers, Mr Guymer and his clubmate Mr Hughes. Mr Guymer, who was unbeaten that season, won the match and cemented his reputation as being the brightest star of the local league. The climax of the evening was an exhibition match given by an England international, named Cohen, and a Welsh international, Jean Morton. In what was described as a very exciting competition the England player won by two games to nil.

Others were looking forward to the football match involving the Scottish Command XI which, while unconfirmed, was sure to feature a range of well-known pre-war players including representatives of clubs such as Aberdeen, Derby County, Dundee, East Fife, Falkirk, Hearts, Hibs, Huddersfield, Partick Thistle, St Johnstone, St Mirren, and Wolverhampton Wanderers. Interest in the match was high and it was certain that a large crowd would be drawn to the spectacle.

As can be seen there were to be several dances throughout the week and the people who had organized the civilian (open) dance were at pains to point out that members of the forces were also welcome to attend as it was recognised that some service personnel would not be able to attend the other dances that were scheduled to take place.

Although Warship Week finished on 30 June, donations continued to pour in for several days afterwards and by the time the final tally was made on 10 June the total stood at £244,400, meaning Orkney had more than doubled its intended target figure. Lord Alness, previously an MP for Orkney, once again sent a telegram of congratulation to the people of the islands for their generosity.

Yet another Orcadian airman lost his life while training in June, Sergeant Jacques Thorfinn Goodsir (22). Sergeant Goodsir lost his life when the engine of his Hurricane I (P3227) caught fire in mid-air and the aircraft crashed near Kirtlebridge in Dumfriesshire on 15 June. At the time Sergeant Goodsir was based at RAF Annan with 55 OTU. An Orcadian, Sergeant Goodsir's father was a former soldier, Lieutenant Colonel James Taylor Goodsir, and his mother, Berthe Marie Constance Goodsir, was French. The family lived at St Margaret's Hope.[36]

RAF Bomber Command was now under its new, determined, commander, Arthur 'Bomber' Harris, and during the summer had undertaken three publicity grabbing 1,000-bomber raids in order to establish the abilities and potential of the, at the time, much-maligned force. Aside from the regular bombing operations on German towns and cities, the aircrew of Bomber Command also mounted extensive sea-mining operations in order to hamper enemy shipping. Typically, the airmen gave a nickname to these operations, calling them 'gardening' ops

Hurricane of 55 OTU in flight. (Public Domain)

while the mines that they dropped were termed 'vegetables'. These missions were often flown during full-moon periods when lengthy trips into occupied Europe were too hazardous, or were used for the purpose of giving inexperienced crews their first familiarity with operations, or to give what was seen as an easier operation to a crew nearing the end of their tour of operations. On the night of 6 / 7 July the command dispatched forty-two aircraft on various 'gardening' operations, three of them, all Wellington bombers, failed to return. Two of these were from 156 Squadron based at RAF Alconbury and one of these was Wellington III (X3345). The aircraft took off from Alconbury at 11.59pm to lay mines in French waters under the command of the pilot, Sergeant A.F. Galley. Nothing more was heard from the crew and they were later confirmed as having crashed in the target area with all five men being killed. The wireless operator / air gunner aboard X3345 was Sergeant John David Robert Heddle (18) of Stromness, the son of Robert S. and Josephine Heddle.[37]

Less than a fortnight after Sergeant Heddle lost his life another Orcadian member of Bomber Command was killed. Yet again, this was a loss which was not due to enemy action but to an accident suffered as a result of a mechanical failure. During the summer of 1942 some of Bomber Command's squadrons were in the course of converting to the powerful four-engine Lancaster bomber and many were flying a greater number of training flights than usual in addition to their operational duties. As a member of 106 Squadron, commanded by the future 'Dam Buster' Wing Commander Guy Gibson, on 21 July Pilot Officer Carlyle, RCAF and his crew took off on a practice bombing sortie in Lancaster I (R5576). The squadron was still in the midst of converting to the Lancaster from the ill-fated Manchester bomber and many pilots had few hours on the new aircraft. Immediately following take off the port inner engine failed and witnesses watched as the massive bomber climbed slowly to 200ft before stalling and crashing near the airfield at RAF Coningsby. All ten men on board, including several ground-crew, were killed. One of several air gunners flying in the crew, presumably to get in some training, was Sergeant Robert Muir Mathieson (21), the son of Donald Sutherland Mathieson and Williamina Muir Mathieson of St Margaret's Hope, South Ronaldsay.[38]

We have heard previously how experienced RAF officer John Honeyman Clouston Harrold (46) had been promoted to the rank of squadron leader while serving in Egypt. Sadly, his parents received news that their son had died on 7 August. At the time of his death, Squadron Leader Harrold had been on attachment to the Royal Air Force of Oman (RAFO).[39]

With the war in the Mediterranean becoming intense in the build-up to Operation Torch, there was an increasing demand for aircraft in the theatre. On 20 August a crew from 15 OTU at RAF Harwell took off to ferry an anti-submarine warfare Wellington VIII (HX566) to Egypt via RAF Portreath and Gibraltar. After landing and refuelling at Portreath the crew took off on the morning of 27 August bound for Gibraltar, but they encountered poor weather conditions and drifted off-track colliding with a hill in Andalusia. The aircraft caught fire and only one of the crew, the rear gunner, Sergeant Rodney Webber, RCAF, survived. The second pilot was Sergeant Leonard Sutherland (21) of Stromness, the son of John William and Helen Sutherland. He was buried along with the other members of the crew at Gibraltar (North Front) Cemetery. There was some confusion amongst the Spanish authorities as to how many men had been killed aboard the Wellington. This was probably explained by the ferocity of the fire and also explains, probably, why no personal effects were forwarded to the families of the deceased.[40]

CHAPTER 5

1943: Turning the Tide

On the last day of January Orkney Agricultural Society held its annual bull show at Kirkwall Auction Mart. The entry of forty Aberdeen Angus bulls was supposedly the best that had ever been seen at the event and the championship was won by Mr A. Calder of Sebay, St Andrews, with a 15-month-old bull named Agrippa Sebay. The reserve champion was the patriotically named 13-month-old bull Defiance of Midhouse, owned by Mr M. Horne of Midhouse, Evie. At the sale, Agrippa Sebay was sold to a Shapinsay farmer for 81 guineas and the reserve champion fetched 91 guineas. Two other bulls fetched more than the champion, one of these was a prize winner and the other one was an also-ran. The show, despite the wartime conditions, attracted a large crowd of farmers drawn from the east and west of the Scottish mainland along with those from the islands. Mr David Flett, the auctioneer, was very pleased with the results of the auction with high prices being met for all of the bulls which were sold.

Just days after the bull show there was a more warlike gathering when the Deputy Civil Defence Commissioner for Orkney and Zetland, Mr H.W. Scarth, organized a meeting of representatives from a variety of civil defence and ARP services in the area at the Municipal Chamber in Kirkwall. Chairing the meeting, Mr Scarth alluded to the times immediately following the Nazi conquest of Norway when the imminent threat to the security of Orkney and Shetland, and therefore indeed the whole of Britain, had necessitated organising themselves and their services for emergency use if an invasion or severe raid came. Mr Scarth told the delegates that he feared another such time was upon them and that it was entirely possible that the summer would once more bring the threat of invasion. As the county controlled the north-eastern passage, the people of Orkney and Shetland must, he insisted, 'give up looking at their county as they knew it before, a pleasant, tranquil place to live in. It had been suddenly transformed into a key position. Without it the task of the Fleet in protecting the Eastern seaboard would be made very hard.'[41] Mr Scarth insisted that his remarks were not intended as scaremongering, but that it was impossible to deny the strategic importance of the county and that although Britain had strengthened herself since the darkest of days, the Germans too had made use of their time and an attempted invasion was still very possible. It was his job to ensure that they were not becoming complacent.

Labouring his point, Mr Scarth went on to outline how it was very likely that the county would, in the near future, suffer a very heavy air attack. While he acknowledged that they had already made great preparations for their services, it was necessary they continue to attend to all of their tasks, large or small, however tiresome they may be. They must in the next few days analyse their organizations, identify any weaknesses and eliminate them. If weaknesses were identified, then Mr Scarth said he would be more than willing to do whatever was in his power to help resolve them.

Continuing, Mr Scarth told the delegates that he was addressing the gathering with some diffidence, as he was aware that many of them were his seniors and that others already had distinguished records of service in the county. However, as the powers of the Regional Commissioners were so vast (in the event of an area being cut off due to invasion or a raid which disabled central government they were expected to be the immediate and all-powerful representative of central government in their area) he felt it his duty to remind them that in the event of the county being cut off he might be expected to give orders in the name of central government and would be relying on men such as themselves to ensure such orders were obeyed without question or hesitation.

Mr Scarth appears to have not only been somewhat diffident, as he claimed, but also somewhat concerned over possible local recalcitrance or even resistance to his, and his superiors', authority.

Following this address the meeting moved on to the discussion of the various organizations and any concerns which the delegates had. Provost J.G. Marwick raised the first concern on behalf of Stromness Town Council. The Provost claimed that the food supplies which were being sent to Stromness were completely inadequate for the much-enlarged wartime population. Mr Scarth replied that owing to the peculiar circumstances which were faced by Orkney and Shetland (i.e. the influx of military personnel increasing the populations substantially) the Board of Trade had agreed with the Regional Commissioner that special consideration would be given to the county, but investigations would have to be undertaken into specific needs with a view to securing extra supplies.

A further question relating to food supplies was posed by the Food Officer, Miss Annie Miller, who asked if the Deputy Commissioner was aware that some traders in the area were in the habit of allowing their reserves of certain foodstuffs to run low and that this had caused shortages. Mr Scarth replied that traders would be advised not to follow this practice through the local Chamber of Commerce.

Worries over a perceived inadequate supply of fire-fighting equipment were next on the agenda, with Provost Marwick and Provost Flett of Kirkwall both querying the supply of equipment for fighting incendiary bombs and agreeing that securing pumps was very difficult. They were answered by Chief Constable Campbell who, in a rather blasé manner, assured the two provosts that he had secured fifty stirrup pumps and assured Mr Scarth that this was sufficient to supply squads in both burghs.

Chief Constable Campbell then gave an update on the ARP services in which he said that the organization had so far proved itself although there was an undoubted shortage of fire appliances. He was able to confidently state that incendiary bombs could be adequately dealt with and that they were fully ready to cope with such devices, although there had been a distinct shortage of volunteers in Stromness which he claimed was by far the worst, along with Kirkwall, in the county. Responding to the new orders for firefighting, i.e. the establishment of fire watchers in business premises, the Chief Constable said that he saw 'no useful purpose being served by business people sitting out night and day in the streets' when they had business to deal with. Rather he proposed that they organise themselves into groups and inform him of the names of their leaders so he could arrange to have them informed of any air raid in advance. He then made it clear he was here talking solely about the two towns of Kirkwall and Stromness, but that in other communities the fire-watch system was already well established and that the watchers had the authority to call out fire-parties. He then added, somewhat mystifyingly, that he 'did not think that was necessary in Kirkwall and Stromness'.[42]

There does appear to have been some confusion over the new fire-fighting regulations, with Provost Flett outlining his concerns over the number of fire-fighting squads in Kirkwall, only to be told by Mr Scarth that business premises had to provide their own fire-fighting squad, but not a 24-hour watch. The Chief Constable added that this only applied to businesses with less than thirty-one employees, while smaller businesses did not have to provide a fire-watch at all. The Town Clerk of Kirkwall, Mr D.M. Wood, then joined the discussion, adding that there were forty-five fire-fighting squads registered in Kirkwall, but that very few were from business premises with the majority being from outside of Albert Street, Bridge Street, Broad Street and Victoria Street. Provost Flett then concluded that it was likely many of those who had joined these squads were themselves businessmen with properties in the unrepresented streets, but had joined squads elsewhere in town where they lived.

We have already seen how the authorities had designated Orkney and Shetland a Protected Area (No.2 Protected Area) as a measure to limit and keep an eye on the numbers of people living in this strategically vital region. The next point raised concerned the apparent failures of this measure and the increased burden this had placed upon local authorities. It was claimed by several representatives that large numbers of people had come to the islands and this was exacerbating the supply situation. The incomers consisted of the families of service personnel who had been posted to the area, of workmen, of others who had been moved to Orkney as a result of the war, and of islanders who had previously moved south but had returned due to wartime conditions in other parts of the country. The problem, it was claimed, applied across the whole of Orkney but was a particular problem in Kirkwall and Stromness.

All of the delegates agreed it was unacceptable that this influx should place additional strains on local facilities which were already overburdened by the demands of wartime. Thus, it was decided to approach the Ministry of Labour and National Service to demand the halting of any further influx into what was supposedly a protected area. A representative from the Ministry then sought to pass the buck by claiming this was, in fact, a matter for the military authorities as it was they who organized and were responsible for the granting of permits. The next to speak on this matter were two local doctors. Dr W.B. Bannerman agreed with the concerns raised as he claimed it was leading to overcrowding in many homes. Dr Hugh Marwick, however, raised concerns that any new measures to stop people entering the area might adversely affect people who had been bombed out. Many of these people, he claimed, were natives of Orkney and he urged care not to exclude this group from returning. Addressing this point, Mr Scarth pointed out that unfortunate people who fell into this category were to be billeted on Shetland.

Identifying one of the weaknesses which he had mentioned earlier, Mr Scarth next raised the issue of communities appointing one central person to oversee the co-ordination of the restoration of essential services such as drainage, electricity, gas and water, along with the clearance of debris after raids, rather than having many different council officers responsible for each task. He raised this point with Kirkwall in mind particularly as 'he would feel happier if they had one co-ordinating individual who would look after all these services'. Responding to this, Provost Flett suggested that the Burgh Surveyor, Mr Oddie, was the right man for the job with the Lord Lieutenant then adding that it would be wise to add a deputy to Mr Oddie in case he was injured during an air raid. Baillie Slater of Kirkwall suggested two council officers, Mr Cooper and Mr Fox, as suitable deputies.

Perhaps nettled by the criticism, Provost Flett then told the gathering that Kirkwall already exhibited a considerable degree of co-operation in such matters and that the current scheme of ARP could immediately switch over to an emergency setting. At this point, Chief Constable Campbell intervened once more to point out that several police officers had already been appointed as incident officers and had responsibility for directing repair squads to where they were needed. He did admit, however, that the system would be benefited by a central co-ordinator. In conclusion, the meeting agreed that it seemed that Mr Oddie was indeed the correct man for the job.

The final point to be raised was that of young Orkadians being drawn away from the island immediately after they finished their schooling by the offer of large wartime wages in unskilled jobs, rather than learning trades which would be of benefit to them after the war. A representative from the Ministry of Labour suggested that the Orkney Education Authority should encourage lads to undertake training in various crafts at contractors' camps which had already been established on the island. He added that it would be necessary to adopt some form of propaganda in order to convince lads that it would be of benefit to themselves to forgo the lure of large wages now in exchange for learning a trade which would be of benefit to them in later life. The chairman of the Orkney Education Committee, Mr John White, answered rather cautiously saying only that he was sure the committee would be willing to consider the matter.

With 100 days to go until the launch of the Wings for Victory campaign the organising committee, under the chairmanship of the redoubtable Provost Flett, announced at the beginning of March that the event would open with the now usual parade and it was hoped that a high-ranking member of the RAF would be present to take the salute. A target figure of £140,000 had been set, with the Kirkwall district setting itself a total contribution of £45,000 towards this figure. Locally, an enthusiastic response had been seen with organising committees having been set up in many areas and campaigns to elicit enthusiasm and to raise involvement continuing apace.

This enthusiasm was in itself a very positive sign for the authorities. Although the tide of war seemed to be changing, elsewhere in Britain there was a growing sense of war weariness as people became increasingly worn down by the constant demands of a country involved in a total war. Rationing, shortages, the blackout, increased workloads and hours and a lack of leisure time or the facilities to use such leisure time, all combined to create a rather grim atmosphere in this fifth year of the war. On Orkney, however, there was little sign of grumbling or a decline in morale. Perhaps helped by the reminder of the ever-present Home Fleet, the Orcadians seem to have adjusted to wartime conditions with remarkably little fuss. True, rationing, while onerous, meant there was a fair share for all available and, with many Orcadians having relatively easy access to wartime treats such as fresh eggs and a steady supply of fish, the people continued in a relatively cheerful and determined mood.

The public enthusiasm for the Wings for Victory campaign was demonstrated once more at the end of March when a publicity show at the Albert Kinema in Kirkwall proved so popular that some people had to be turned away. The meeting, a part of the St Ola publicity campaign, featured several RAF themed films along with one which explored the scuttling of the German fleet at Scapa at the end of the First World War. Speakers for the night were Provost Flett and Mr Frank Illingworth of the Ministry of Information. A collection raised over £9 for the campaign.

One of the reasons for the popularity of the Wings for Victory campaign and the RAF was that many people were reading or listening to daily news items which related how the RAF was hitting back at Germany, largely through the operations of Bomber Command. For many it seemed, unfairly, that the RAF was the only force which was in fact hitting back at the Germans and support for the force was, therefore, at an all-time high at this phase in the war. Orcadians also had four aerodromes on their doorsteps and the activities of RAF Coastal Command in patrolling the waters around Orkney were ever-present reminders of the contribution that the RAF was making to the war effort.

The men of the Home Guard continued in their duties throughout the year, even though the threat of invasion or

A sloop off the Old Man of Hoy. (The Sphere)

even raiding had decreased markedly. The Home Guard was now becoming far better equipped and its members provided a very valuable service in undertaking duties which released regular soldiers for more vital commissions and in providing training for youngsters who were yet to be called up. The Home Guard also provided many men with a busy social life in which they believed they were actively contributing to the war effort. April saw the Orkney Home Guard form its own pipe band and the newly inaugurated group was present at a large parade on Sunday, 11 April. The men of the Home Guard, led by Major Bruce, marched past a saluting stand on Broad Street, where the Lord Lieutenant and Lieutenant-Colonel Brown took the salute. Before the parade the men of the Home Guard had attended a series of Army Cinematograph Service training films, including one entitled 'Desert Victory', which the management of the Albert Kinema had agreed to show free of charge.

With the threat of war weariness, it was vital that Orcadians had events and facilities that could provide leisure opportunities. This was helped by the fact that many of the communities were already largely used to providing their own entertainment and numerous small musical gatherings and such continued throughout the war. In Kirkwall there were even more facilities available with the Albert Kinema proving very popular throughout the wartime years. In mid-April cinema-goers could enjoy features such as 'King Arthur was a Gentleman', 'Meet John Dee', 'Reap the Wild Wind' (featuring John Wayne), 'Dr Jekyll and Mr Hyde', or, for the younger generation, Mickey Mouse in 'Mickey's Birthday Party'.

As Easter approached there were several more events of a more spiritual nature. Paterson Church offered a performance of Handel's 'Messiah' performed by the church choir, while St Magnus Cathedral offered an organ recital. At Bridge Street Wynd the Kirkwall Corps of the Salvation Army held special Easter services on 23-25 April. At 7.30pm on Good Friday (23 April) the programme was 'The Seven Sayings of Jesus' and 'Two Hours at the Cross' conducted by Brigadier Buck and his wife. The couple had only recently arrived in the north of Scotland from Newcastle-upon-Tyne after being appointed to undertake duties in the north. The Easter week would be marked by their first visit to Orkney and a hearty welcome was expected, as had already been the case when they visited Aberdeen, Inverness, Findochty and Thurso.

The following evening saw a musical programme with refreshments and on Easter Sunday the message was delivered in services at 11.15am, 3pm and 7pm. No doubt many of the Orcadians took advantage of these services and others which were organized for 22 April, which had been declared a public holiday. With the huge numbers of service personnel on Orkney it was impossible for all those who wished to attend an Easter service to pack themselves into the islands' churches. On Good Friday an open-air service for service personnel was held in front of St Magnus Cathedral. It took place at 8pm and was conducted by the Rev. P. Marrow, RAF, assisted by speakers from all three services with the theme of 'Calvary is Victory'. The event was widely publicised with all servicemen and women, as well as civilians, being invited to attend.

Other Orcadians were more concerned with ensuring they could grow sufficient food for themselves and their families. In this endeavour they were assisted by regular columns in the press which gave hints and tips on growing vegetables and rearing stock such as pigs and poultry. One of the most popular and long-running columns in the *Orkney Herald* was 'Vegetables for Victory' by George E. Greenhowe of the North of Scotland College for Agriculture. His mid-April column provided hints on the sowing of early carrots, giving instructions on how to sow the carrots and also advice on which varieties were best suited. The column also advised that cauliflowers and Brussels sprouts which had been grown on in cold frames could now be planted out. Mr Greenhowe also advised on how a small sowing of early Milan turnips could be planted between rows of broad beans or rows marked out for sprouts. He also cautioned that it would be beneficial to plant more leeks this year than had been the norm so that adequate supplies would be available in winter and the spring of 1944.

With such a large number of servicemen present on the islands relations could sometimes be strained and there seems to have been a problem in Kirkwall with servicemen harassing women on the streets after dark. One letter writer contacted the *Orkney Herald* under the pen name 'Messenger' to address this issue. After complaining over the shape of the helmets issued to fire guards, the writer moved on to the issue of performing her duties after dark. She asked whether the authorities expected female fire guards to patrol the dark streets and said that, while she would do anything to help in the event of an air raid during daylight hours, she would not be willing to go out in Kirkwall at night until the authorities 'manage to stop soldiers and sailors shouting after and running after women in the dark' and would not be willing to undertake her duties in the blackout.[43]

Although Orkney was geographically isolated, the residents had no doubt that they were completely involved in the war effort. The presence of the Home Fleet, the four aerodromes and the proximity of a large Army contingent were constant reminders of the war. Orcadians were also updated on the conduct of the war through regular articles in the local press. The spring saw articles on the growing strength of the Bomber Command campaign. The air correspondent of the *Orkney Herald* told readers how the nightly raids were growing in strength and intensity and were causing an increasing level of devastation in German towns and cities, resulting in a serious impact on the German economy and its industry. The reporter stated that a 'neutral estimate of the direct and indirect effect of this bombing is a drop of 30 per cent in German output'.[44] What was more, the heavy and persistent raids by both British and American bombers were seriously disrupting Germany's transport systems, with the dislocation causing great concern amongst the Nazi commanders.

Some Orcadians had been questioning why there had been no further 1,000-bomber raids such as those which had taken place in the previous year. The answer was two-fold. Assembling a fleet of 1,000 bombers had been a tremendously taxing undertaking involving the use of not just the whole of Bomber Command's frontline strength, but also the aircraft of the training units, day-bomber squadrons and even some which were donated by other commands. Secondly, the command's improving equipment and aircraft now meant that a higher tonnage of bombs could be dropped by fewer aircraft, while the creation of 8 (Pathfinder Force) Group had also enabled them to achieve greater accuracy. The reporter informed his readers that the 1,000-bomber raids had been a successful experiment, but that subsequent attempts to build up Bomber Command quickly had been frustrated by the need for some of its aircraft to be diverted to Coastal Command duties.

Nevertheless, the introduction of the new four-engine bombers, the Stirling, Halifax and Lancaster, meant that a force of just 300 bombers was able to deliver a bombload equivalent to that delivered during a 1,000-bomber raid. The reporter illustrated this point by comparing the Armstrong Whitworth Whitley (a main part of the force from 1939-1942) to the newly introduced Avro Lancaster. While the Whitley had a cruising speed of 160-180 mph and could carry 6,000lbs of bombs, the Lancaster could carry three times the bombload, could fly at greater altitude and was faster than the Whitley. The 1,000-bomber raids might be repeated once again, assured the reporter, but the tonnage of bombs would be far greater than the 1,500 tons of bombs dropped on Cologne by 1,000 bombers in 1942 and many of the bombs would be the new 8,000lb bombs which had recently caused great destruction in Germany. Thus the people of Orkney were kept informed about developments in the air war, while also being subtly encouraged to back the efforts of the RAF.

As the Wings for Victory campaign approached, a mobile film unit was touring the islands showing various films linked to the RAF and the campaign. On 6 June, for example, the unit stopped at the Stromness Town Hall and large crowds flocked to see the films on offer. At each stop the film unit made a collection for the campaign using collecting boxes labelled for the specific districts in which the funds were raised. The day before the Stromness show the unit had stopped at the, soon to be opened, Strond Cinema at St Mary's Village and had once more proved to be extremely popular.

From 8-11 June one of the main attractions of the Wings for Victory campaign was the show 'Wings over Orkney', which was put on by members of the RAF, including a number of WAAFs, stationed locally. This was a variety performance with a difference in that it consisted of a large number of original sketches and performances created especially for the show. The show proved to be a great success, falling behind only the official ENSA shows in terms of the amount of interest it aroused, and local reviews stated confidently that the show would be 'remembered for at least a generation to come'.[45]

On 19 June the opening ceremony for the Wings for Victory campaign saw huge crowds in attendance with the RAF really getting behind the effort. Along with a decorated saluting dais on the edge of Market Green there was a modern fighter aircraft, a power-operated gun turret and a selection of bombs on Market Green for people to inspect. The committee had promised to solicit the presence of a prominent member of the RAF and it delivered, with Air Vice Marshal Raymond Collishaw CB DSO OBE DSC DFC being present to take the salute. AVM Collishaw had been the highest-scoring fighter pilot of the Royal Naval Air Service (RNAS) during the First World War and had remained in the RAF. From 1939 to 1941 he had been the commanding officer of 204 Group in North Africa and had seen that command through a very difficult period when it was woefully ill-equipped to carry the fight to the Italian and German forces. Brought back home in 1941 he had then been posted as senior officer in Fighter Command on Orkney. With his past connections to the RN, and his current posting, he had a very good knowledge of the islands and was a popular figure.[46]

A crowd of 6,000 people crammed into Broad Street and Market Green to witness the opening ceremony. Once again, the Lord Lieutenant presided over the event and read a selection of telegrams of encouragement which had been received. A number of dignitaries were present on the saluting dais and the first of these called to speak was the Joint Under Secretary of State for Scotland, Mr Allan Chapman MP. Beginning by saying that the most important speaker was Air Vice Marshal Collishaw, Mr Chapman went on to express his gratitude to the people of Orkney for the warmth of his welcome during his brief tour, which was concluding that day, and for the steady support they had determinedly given the war effort. Mr Chapman said that he saw the farmers of Orkney as a symbol of the nation's determination. The farmers on the islands had 'wrested rough land from the hillsides and brought those acres under cultivation'. Given the support for the war effort on Orkney he believed that the Orcadians would, once again, exceed the target which they had set for themselves. Instilling a sense of rivalry and competition, Mr Chapman added that he had just come from Shetland where he had witnessed their now highly successful Wings for Victory campaign, but was reassured that Orcadians were 'prepared to take up challenges from all-comers'.[47] Reiterating the debt owed by Britain to the RAF Mr Chapman said that they had won freedom for the country by winning the Battle of Britain, had paved the way for victory in the desert, and were taking the offensive to the enemy in his own lands.

Air Vice Marshal Collishaw gave a rather terse and short speech to open the campaign, saying that, as the Prime Minister had commented recently, it was unknown just what the RAF could achieve during the war, but it was hoped that they could bring about the breakdown of the enemy's will to fight through its sustained bombing campaigns and that the Orkney Wings Victory campaign was an important part of that. As a bugler played the Reveille the indicator on the Market Green was run up to the sum achieved so far: £37,580. The highlight of the day was the parade consisting of almost 2,000 men and women representing the forces, ARP and civil defence organizations.

Order of March for Wings for Victory Opening Ceremony Parade

Argyll & Sutherland Highlanders Band
RAF & RAF Regiment (300 members)
WAAF (90)
ATC (60)
Girls' Training Corps (40)
Band of the Royal Marines
Royal Navy (80)
WRNS (60)
Royal Marines (60)
Highland Regiment pipe band
Anti-Aircraft Detachment (100)
Company of Highland Infantry
ATS (100)
Home Guard Pipe Band
Home Guard (100)
Army Cadet Force (80)
Highland Regiment Pipe Band
Warden Service (50)
First Aid and Reserve Service
WVS
National Fire Service (NFS)
Kirkwall Burgh Fire Guard
Boys' Brigade and Life Boys
Girl Guides
Brownies

The platform erected in Broad Street for the saluting stand was retained and used as a bandstand for two open air variety concerts, which included musical performances and a display

Wings for Victory Campaign Poster. (Orkney Herald)

of Scottish country dancing organized by Mrs Skea. On 22 June the main performers were the 'Sunshine Party' while on 25 June the headliners were the very popular Bignold Park Concert Party led by Squadron Leader Fox.

Once again there was the now usual variety of shows, events and galas which marked the savings campaigns. People were endlessly inventive, with small groups organising events such as raffles and whist drives in order to raise funds, while others held small recitals and concerts in a variety of the small communities around Orkney.

The Wings for Victory campaign was noted for the contributions made by the locally stationed members of all three of the armed services. We have already seen how the RAF ran a very successful variety concert tour and now the Royal Navy also put on a similar show at the Naval Cinema. Opening the naval concert, Provost Flett informed the audience that although the original total set for Kirkwall was £45,000, it had been decided, in light of the enthusiasm being shown and the amount already raised, to increase this to £60,000. The War Weapons week in 1941 had been set at a rate of £5 per head, the Warships Week of 1942 at £6 per head and both of these had been handsomely exceeded. Therefore the rate of £7 per head had been set for the Wings for Victory campaign.

By the end of the campaign the people of Orkney could once again be extremely proud of their efforts with the sum of £299,221 being raised. Notably, this included £4,138 in free gifts and a further £1,000 in interest-free loans.

The final day, Saturday, 26 June, saw a closing ceremony held in Kirkwall. The town had been quiet all day as many people were attending the Scottish Command v Combined Services football match taking place at Hatston Farm. By early evening, however, many of the 3,000 who had attended the game made their way to Kirkwall and the streets became busy. Following a pipe band performance, a simple closing ceremony was performed from the stand on Broad Street at which the semi-final total was announced to much acclaim. This was in turn followed by a large street auction sale conducted by Mr David S. Flett of Messrs T. Smith Peace of Kirkwall Auction Mart.

Speaking to the crowd, Provost Flett stated his joy at the effort which had been put into the campaign. He informed the crowd that Orkney had now contributed approximately £2,000,000 since the start of the war and that this represented savings of £100 per head of the pre-war population. Commenting on the free gifts portion of the sum, Provost Flett said that he was astonished by the generosity of Orcadians. In 1942 some £1,200 had been given to the Warships Week campaign in free gifts, but this time that total had been exceeded by thousands of pounds.

Day-by-Day Totals for Orkney Wings for Victory Campaign

Date (June)	Time	Total (£)
19th	pm	37,580
21st	1pm	57,250
	8pm	67,562

22nd	1pm	91,841
	8pm	111,613
23rd	1pm	119,975
	8pm	129,173
24th	1pm	141,656
	8pm	152,651
25th	1pm	165,908
	8pm	189,030
26th	Noon	217,772
	9pm	277,405
28th	pm	299,221

In July Orcadians were reminded that, despite the apparent shift in the nation's fortunes in the war, Britain's supply lines were still over-stretched and that shortages were to remain a commonplace of wartime life. It was announced that the clothing ration was, once again, to be cut for the coming year. For the many Orcadians who were employed in labour intensive jobs such as agriculture or the fishing industry, this was another blow as their clothing wore out more quickly than those who enjoyed more sedate employment. The changes, however, were accepted with a stoic attitude and remarkably little grumbling was evident on Orkney in the days following the announcement.

From August Orkney became one of the main bases for the Arctic Convoys taking aid to the Soviet Union. By the end of the war some 1,400 merchant vessels and their extensive number of escort vessels had ferried essential supplies and wartime matériel to the ports of Archangel and Murmansk for the loss of 85 merchantmen and 16 warships. The people of Orkney became used to the presence of the men who manned these convoys, which took place under brutal weather conditions and carried great risk.

For Orkney farmers October brought a stern reminder not to waste precious stores of winter livestock feed. Although supplies had been maintained, the restrictions on imports and the effects

Arctic Convoy Memorial on Orkney. (Irene Moore)

of losses continuing to be suffered in the Battle of the Atlantic meant that such supplies as were available were not to be used for purposes which would have been perfectly normal during pre-war days, but were now considered to be squandered resources.

Arctic Convoy Memorial plaque. (Irene Moore)

For the coming winter, farmers were informed, protein would be in short supply, but this would be somewhat balanced by the greater availability of cereals. As with most aspects of wartime Britain the supply of such materials was strongly enforced and the government issued guidelines for farmers. For dairy cows, for example, four units (1 protein and 3 cereal) were to be allotted for every 100 gallons of milk sold in excess of 15 gallons per cow per month. There was, however, a cereal deduction of 48lbs per cow per month, calculated on milk sales from two months' previously. This deduction could be waived if 3cwt of oats or dredge corn per cow had been sold. There were a number of adjustments which could be made to these figures for winter milk producers who had a high proportion of autumn and early winter calvers in their herds. For those who kept no more than two cows for producing milk for the household, and where no rations were issued per milk sales, a monthly allowance of ¼ unit of protein could be applied for.

Those farmers who relied on horsepower for their work were reminded that growing winter feed for these horses was to be a priority, but for those who could not produce enough winter feed then rations would be allowed, depending on proof being confirmed, at a maximum of four units per horse involved in heavy and continuous work. In addition, a half unit of bran could be secured by the sale of a similar quantity of oats.

For poultry keepers one unit was issued for every 160 birds, while pig keepers (and there were many who became wartime pig keepers) received one unit for every eight pigs. Once again there were deductions. For pigs this deduction was at the rate of one unit for every 8 acres while for poultry keepers it was set at three units for every 40 acres. Where both pigs and poultry were kept on the same farm the rate was set at one unit for every 10 acres. A further ration of three units was allowed for each breeding sow or gilt which was about to farrow.

For those growing oats, beans and peas (Orkney farmers, like many others, had been encouraged to bring otherwise unproductive land into arable and vegetable production) and who sold such large quantities for seed that they were left with insufficient supplies to feed their own livestock, additional coupons could be applied for in order to enable them to meet the needs of their stock.

The local War Agricultural Committees (War Ags) had previously had quantities of feed placed under their charge for issue at their own discretion, but farmers were informed that in 1943 this quantity would be substantially reduced and that protein, in particular, would be in very short supply. Farmers were warned that, although the War Ags would make every attempt to satisfy demand it might not be possible and that, in some situations, applications which were worthy might even have to be turned down due to lack of supplies.

CHAPTER 6

1944: D-Day and Beyond

The war in Italy and the Balkans continued apace and on 7 January the campaign took the life of yet another airman with Orkney connections. Flight Sergeant Robert Dickson Kelly, the son of John and Isabella Kelly, was married to Anna Kelly of Stromness. Based with 255 Squadron flying Bristol Beaufighter VIs on night intruder operations over the Balkans, including attacks on shipping on the River Danube, Flight Sergeant Kelly was to undertake a night patrol in Beaufighter VI (MM864) on the night of 7 / 8 January, but he and his navigator, Sergeant Thomas William Waters, were both killed when their aircraft crashed on take-off. Flight Sergeant Kelly was buried at Bari War Cemetery where his next-of-kin had the following inscription placed upon his headstone, 'HE DIED OUR HOMELAND TO DEFEND, A BRITISH AIRMAN'S NOBLE END.'

Every segment of Orcadian society was affected by the war with most families having loved ones serving in the forces, the Merchant Navy or the fishing fleet. Orkney's MP, Mr B.H.H. Neven-Spence, set an example of this commitment to service as he had three children in the forces. His son, Neven Neven-Spence was a second lieutenant in the Parachute Regiment while his two daughters were also serving; Sunniva Neven-Spence in the WAAF and Annette Neven-Spence in the WRNS, where she assisted Winston Churchill at the Quebec Conference.

The children of Orkney's MP. (The Talter)

With food shortages and supplies still at severe risk, Orcadians were repeatedly encouraged to try to grow as much of their own food as possible. A series of campaigns were launched to further this aim, the most famous, of course, being 'Dig for Victory'. The Scottish Gardens and Allotments Committee, the Department of Agriculture for Scotland, the Ministry of Food and the SWRI, maintained a van which toured the country, manned by an expert on vegetable gardening and a qualified cook and nutritionist. The van had been in use for several years but had never crossed to Orkney until May 1944. Although the vehicle was specially equipped, when it arrived at Kirkwall the weather was very poor and the demonstrations had to be relocated to the grammar school. Miss Harrison, the gardening expert, gave a very practical talk on the growing of vegetables and urged all to grow more of these valuable foods. She also introduced a wartime film which described how vegetables and the gardener were on the front lines in this war. Cook and nutritionist, Miss Gillies, gave a very good demonstration of vegetable cooking techniques and showed a film on fruit bottling. Both women afterwards answered a series of questions posed by the large audience.

While the people of Orkney were now used to the ever-popular ENSA concerts alongside the local efforts of civilian and military concert parties, May saw a highly successful tour launched under the auspices of the Council for the Encouragement of Music and the Arts (CEMA). The tour played at communities across Orkney and in every location the audience was left delighted. The tour was composed of several famous Scottish singers and musicians including Horace Fellows (violin), Peggie Sampson (cello), B. Wright Henderson (piano), John Tainsh (tenor) and Marie Thomson (soprano). The performances in Kirkwall were particularly well-attended, but elsewhere numbers were slightly impacted by the activities on offer due to youth week. Cinemagoers, however, were left disappointed by the news that the Albert Kinema was to be closed for much of June for refurbishment.

For those seeking rather more active entertainment, the inter-services boxing tournament held at the Naval Cinema in Lyness proved popular. Many of the audience had turned out following the

Jimmy Wilde. (Orkney Herald)

announcement that prizes would be presented by the former flyweight champion of the world, Jimmy Wilde.

The 'Vegetables for Victory' column in May described, amongst other tips and hints, how to use and prepare liquid manure. This, he wrote, must always be diluted to the appearance of weak tea and when being applied should not touch the foliage. While the most effective manure came from the farm manure heap, when this was not available it was perfectly feasible to make one's own. To do this, advised the column, a bucketful of cow manure or sheep droppings could be suspended, enclosed in a close mesh sack, in a large vessel containing rain water for a few days. Guano could also be employed as a liquid manure by dissolving three ounces in ten gallons of water.

June brought great excitement to the people of Orkney as news broke that the Allies had successfully landed in Normandy. Although anticipation had been growing for many months, the people of Orkney now felt that the final stage of the war was underway. Fittingly, the savings campaign for the year was themed as 'Salute the Soldier' week and would run in late June. By D-Day itself, plans for the week-long campaign were well advanced with preliminary dances and other social functions, including a baby show, having already taken place in many districts. One of the main supporters of the campaign was the pipe band of the 1st Orkney Battalion, Home Guard. Led by Drum Major David Horne, the band had paraded through Kirkwall and Stromness and planned similar performances at Holm and many other districts.

As was now, usual the campaign was to be opened by a parade through Kirkwall with guest of honour, Major General J.N. Slater, officer commanding Orkney and Shetland defences, taking the salute in Broad Street. Other features of the week included a concert by the band of the Royal Scottish Fusiliers in the Albert Kinema, an exhibition of wartime pictures at the Town Council Chambers in Kirkwall, a play by the RAF Players at Bignold Park, military demonstrations, a civil defence parade, a hill race at Wideford, a fancy-dress cycle parade, a mystery motor run and picnic leaving from Stromness, flag days, a drumhead service, a display of ammunition, six-a-side football, a fancy-dress parade, a bring-and-buy sale, a garden fete at Stanger's Dock, and a variety of dances at several locations. These formal events were also bolstered by a plethora of smaller, more locally organized, events varying from whist drives to sports competitions and matches. Amongst the sporting events were the usual inter-service football matches and a netball match between teams from the WAAF and ATS. Of a more martial nature was the rifle shooting competition held between members of the Home Guard at their headquarters.

On 23 June the Home Guard pipe band made the journey to Longhope to take part in the final rally of its tour of the islands. The band travelled across Scapa Flow from Long Houton and played a vigorous selection of music as they marched to the Church of Scotland Hall. The band also played at a children's party for the pupils of South Walls Public School, with Pipe-Major J. Cumming and Piper William MacLeod supplying the music for the Highland dancing.

Once again Orkney had succeeded in smashing its targets for the savings week campaign. When the final total was announced on 20 June the lord lieutenant could proudly state that the sum of £265,882 had been raised during the week-long campaign.

By September the massive construction efforts to build the Orkney barriers had been completed and the moorings at Scapa Flow were made far safer for the Home Fleet as a result. The effort had taken four years and had required a huge expenditure in terms of manpower.

Although rationing was supposed to result in a fair share of food being available for all it was a complex system and was open to contravention by the unscrupulous. In September Orkney Sheriff Court heard two interesting cases involving the contravention of the rationing regulations. The first involved a Finstown merchant named William Stanley Firth, who was charged with having obtained points-rationed food in excess of his allowance by some 3,429 points, with the offences occurring

1944: D-DAY AND BEYOND 121

A stretch of one of the barriers. (Unknown)

*One of the barriers just a month after VE Day. (*The Sphere*)*

between 29 May and 25 June 1944. Mr James Flett, defending, said that although his client pleaded guilty, the oversight was due to a shortage of staff meaning that regulating purchases in accord with his points account was extremely difficult. Although the offence carried a possible sentence of up to six months' imprisonment, a fine of up to £100 or both, Sheriff-Substitute Sutherland Graeme took a lenient view of this first offence on Orkney and fined Mr Firth the sum of just £1.

The second case was not a first offence. Kirkwall general merchant and trader in bacon, James Magnus Moar, had appeared before the bench before but on this occasion was charged with having obtained between 62-86lbs of bacon when his buying permit entitled him to just 31lbs per month. The offence had taken place between 24 January and 28 February 1944 and Mr Moar pleaded not guilty to the charge. After hearing the evidence in the case Sheriff-Substitute Sutherland Graeme found Mr Moar guilty as charged and fined him £5.

The residents of Kirkwall were somewhat alarmed by a series of loud bangs during September, leading some to believe that a flying bomb had landed on the town. Fortunately, this was not the case and it was quickly explained that the source of the noise was the oldest combustion engine in use in the town. The engine was used at the saw and flooring mills of Messrs W.B. Peace & Son at Junction Road. The engine had first come to Kirkwall in 1895 and was now backfiring as a result of the poor quality of wartime gas on Orkney.

By late 1944 the Allied air superiority was such that Bomber Command had once more begun to undertake massed daylight raids. With the failure of Operation Market Garden, however, the Allied right flank near Nijmegen was left vulnerable. On 7 October Bomber Command thus launched raids on the towns of Kleve and Emmerich, which stood on the approach roads to Nijmegen (other attacks took place on the sea walls at Walcheren, while 617 Squadron launched an attack on the Kembs Dam which it was believed the Germans could use to flood the Rhine Valley should the Allies advance). The attack on Emmerich consisted of 340 Lancasters and 110 Mosquitoes and was very accurate with almost 2,500 buildings in the town being destroyed and 680,000 cubic feet of rubble having to be later removed from the town for the loss of only three of the attacking aircraft (all Lancasters).

Amongst the aircraft which failed to return was Lancaster I (PD239, AS-Z) of 166 Squadron. The bomber had taken off from RAF Kirmington shortly before noon with Flight Lieutenant G.U. Pulford at the controls, but nothing more was heard and the crew were declared missing. The mid-upper gunner in the crew was Sergeant William Skea, a 19-year old Orcadian from Northill, Shapinsay. His parents, William and Mary Ann Skea, were informed that their son had failed to return from operations and nothing more was heard of him. A year later his parents placed a notice in the *Orkney Herald* stating that their son had now been officially presumed to have lost his life on 7 October 1944. At some point afterwards the young air gunner's body must have been recovered as he and his entire crew are buried in the Reichswald War Cemetery, Germany.[48]

CHAPTER 7

1945: Peace at Last

Mystery surrounds the death of Corporal Georgina Harcus Mason, WAAF. Corporal Mason was aged 35 when she died on 7 April and had previously been mentioned in despatches in the 1942 New Year's Honours List. Her parents, George and Christina Mason, lived at Stromness, but there is no mention of her in any newspapers of the period and she is buried at Inveresk Parish Churchyard, Midlothian.[49]

Although many hard days lay ahead it was clear that the end was in sight for Germany and many people began to look towards the future. For Orcadians, however, the situation remained much the same with rationing and other wartime measures still being in place along with the shortages and the bleakness of living in wartime Britain.

When VE Day dawned it was to heavy, incessant rain. This meant that few of the islanders were able to enjoy the flags and bunting which had been put out and most celebrated indoors over the course of the two-day holiday. On the evening of VE Day itself, a service of thanksgiving was held at the Church of Scotland but the inclement weather prevented many people from attending. One Eday family had even more reason than most to rejoice as Mr and Mrs Tulloch of Dale, Westside, received news that their third son, Private Thomas Tulloch, who had been taken prisoner by the Germans following Dunkirk, was now back in Britain and would soon be home.

On North Ronaldsay flags were hoisted early on the morning of VE Day. Although 8 and 9 May had been declared a school holiday, the children still assembled at school as normal. Following a brief thanksgiving service and the singing of 'Land of our Birth' and the National Anthem, the children were addressed by Mrs Scott. They were told that they must remember all of those who would not return, along with those who had been injured physically or mentally as well as those who had lost loved ones. The future was in the hands of the children and they must do their best to ensure a future world where war was impossible. Following this, the children marched to salute the flag before giving three hearty cheers for the victory and were then dismissed to take part in the festivities. There was a large turnout, despite the pouring rain, for the thanksgiving service which was held at the Old Church on the evening of VE Day. Addressing the congregation, Mr J.W. Mackay said that just as they had put every endeavour into supporting the war effort, so they 'must exert every effort to make the years of peace worthy of those who had given so much for us'.[50]

On the second day of the celebrations the main attraction for many was a celebration and dance held at the Memorial Hall. The event had been organized by joint leader of the youth club, Mr John D. Mackay, and a large number of people attended. There was a varied programme of events and during an intermission the attendees, led by the Scouts and Guides, marched to Kirk Brae where a large bonfire was lit by Dr Hector. Mr William Scott of Cavan had ensured that there was a goodly supply of fireworks, rockets, squibs and flares and, following the bonfire celebration and firework display, the crowd marched back to the hall where the dance continued into the early hours.

Days after the end of the war in Europe the Orkney barriers were formally opened on 12 May. Work on the barriers had begun in 1940 following the shock of the loss of the HMS *Royal Oak* and it had been a mammoth undertaking with, at times, in excess of 2,000 workers, including many Italian prisoners of war, working on the complex project. Even though the works were completed after the threat from Germany had ended, they did improve road links in the islands and undoubtedly made the mooring safer for any future war.

While the war with Germany was over, the war with Japan went on with many Orcadian families still suffering an anxious time over loved ones who were still involved in the fighting. At least two Orcadian soldiers, or at least soldiers with Orkney connections, lost their lives fighting against the Japanese after VE Day. Private David Rendall was a 36-year-old Orcadian who had emigrated to Australia where he had joined up and found himself posted to the 2 / 20th Battalion, Australian Infantry. Private Rendall was killed in action fighting against the Japanese and is commemorated on the Labuan Memorial in Malaysia. He was the son of Thomas and Elizabeth Rendall of Orkney. The other casualty was a member of the Royal Artillery. Gunner George Partner (35) was the son of Isaac and Abigail Partner and married to Sarah Swanney Partner of Kirkwall. Gunner Partner lost his life while serving with the 95th Battery, 48th Light Anti-Aircraft Regiment, and is also buried at the Labuan War Cemetery.

On 10 August the people of North Ronaldsay held a particularly joyous meeting of the Youth Club at the Memorial Hall. The occasion was the return of Private John Tulloch, King's Own Scottish Borderers, on leave from Burma and the departure of four members of the club to take up their studies at Kirkwall Grammar School and one at Edinburgh University. Music on the violin and bagpipes was provided by Mr Sydney Scott, while a tea was served by club members. The evening also included a quiz, which the ladies' team won by a few points, and the singing of 'Auld Lang Syne'.

The children attended school where a short thanksgiving service was followed by the dismissal so that the two-day victory holiday could be enjoyed. Most children immediately began collecting items for the bonfire which was being raised on the Kirk Brae. The tractors of Messrs Roy Scott and James Craigie aided in the construction of the bonfire, while ladies of the island collected and prepared the refreshments for the dance and tea to be held later in the day. Around midnight the groups left the hall for the Kirk Brae where the bonfire was lit by Miss Maimie Tulloch. Despite the heavy mist which hung in the air, the bonfire quickly lit the scene and, with fireworks, helped to bring about a party atmosphere. A notable feature of the night were the many lights shining from windows which were no longer blacked out. At Mildam a large crescent formed from electric bulbs was illuminated and Cruesbreck was floodlit. After the festivities at the fire people made their way to the Memorial Hall to complete the celebrations with a victory dance.

At Stromness the news of victory seems to have come as a surprise to some. Most learned of it by the noise of people celebrating in the streets throughout the night and early into the morning. Huge numbers of fireworks were fired into the night sky in far greater numbers than had been the case on VE Day. The citizens and shopkeepers extended the two-day holiday to three days, taking the Friday off as well due to the two-day period falling on a public holiday in the first place. Unfortunately, mist and torrential rain did put a damper on some of the celebrations, but the flags were once more put up, again, in far greater numbers than on VE Day. A large bonfire was constructed on the summit of Brinkie's Brae which included twenty barrels of tar and people had laboured to build it all day. It was to have been lit by a local 'bigwig' but some youths let their high spirits carry them away and set a match to the fire earlier in the evening which somewhat spoiled the effect and the youths faced the wrath of those who had endeavoured to build the fire. At the South End, near Hopedale, an unofficial bonfire of some size was also set ablaze. As a result of this fire a tar barrel burst open in Ness Road causing a considerable mess. The celebrations were accompanied by the explosions of yet more fireworks. A united service of thanksgiving was also held at Victoria Street Church which attracted a considerable congregation despite the foul weather.

On the following day the weather improved, but the town was far quieter with most people choosing to celebrate quietly with friends and family although there was an open-air dance held at the North Pier.

The people of Orkney awoke on 15 August to find that VJ Day was upon them and the war was finally over. Unfortunately, the weather was still poor with heavy and continuous rainfall marring many of the planned events. The Gala Day intended for Bignold Park was forced into a last-minute switch to the Grammar School. Nevertheless, the 300 children enjoyed the festivities with games and singing and an apparently inexhaustible supply of food and drink. Despite the weather the fancy-dress competition still managed to attract twenty entrants with the winners being Arthur John Stevens and Brenda Johnston. The baby show was, once again, a success with forty entrants in the four sections of the contest. The winners were: Dennis Muir (1-6 months); Catherine Mowatt (6-12 months); Sandra Allum (12-18 months) and Margaret Scott (18-24 months). The dance which was held in the Town Hall was a great success with the music of the Orphir Band, under the leadership of Alan Anderson, proving very popular. Costa, Evie, celebrated the news with a bonfire and dance held on the hill of Vinquin, while the dance moved inside to the hut at Arsdale.

For the first time since September 1939 the people of Orkney found themselves at peace. Many were still separated from loved ones who were serving abroad or elsewhere in Britain, but for the vast majority it was a time for celebration combined with reflection for those who had lost their lives or been maimed during the course of the war. There were also fears and hopes over what the future might hold for the people of the islands.

However, there was one more tragedy. There is something of a mystery concerning the death of another Orcadian, Gunner William M. McDonald (21) of the 96th (Royal 1st Devon Yeomanry) Field Regiment, Royal Artillery, who died in Malaysia with his death being recorded as having occurred on 26 May 1946. The son of Alexander Henderson McDonald and Marion McDonald of Holm, he is buried at the Kuala Lumpur (Cheras Road) Cemetery.

Endnotes

1. HMS *Courageous* had begun life as a Courageous-class cruiser and had been launched in 1916 before taking part in the final two years of the First World War. Due to naval treaty rules she was converted into an aircraft carrier with the work being complete by 1928.
2. Oddly, Seaman Sutherland is not to be found on the CWGC website lists of the dead. It is possible he was not listed as his death was in an accident, but this seems unlikely. There is a RNR seaman named Sutherland listed as having lost his life on the south coast in October, but he is named as John William Sheppard Sutherland of the armed yacht HMS *Sir Charles McIver*.
3. There are many accounts of the sinking of the *Royal Oak* but for an account of this disaster along with the contradictory evidence mentioned above see McKee, Alexander, *Black Saturday. The Royal Oak Tragedy at Scapa Flow* (Cerberus, 2004) or H.J. Weaver, *Nightmare at Scapa Flow. The Truth About The Sinking of HMS Royal Oak* (Birlinn, 2015).
4. McKee, Alexander, *Black Saturday. The Royal Oak Tragedy at Scapa Flow* (Cerberus, 2004), p.92.
5. *Orkney Herald, and Weekly Advertiser and Gazette for the Orkney & Zetland Islands*, 3 January 1940, p.4.
6. *The Scotsman*, 25 May 1940, p.10.
7. *Orkney Herald*, 3 January 1940, p.5.
8. Seaman Bruce is commemorated on the Lowestoft Memorial. By the end of the war his parents, Alexander and Mary Jane Walls Bruce, were living at St Margaret's Hope, South Ronaldsay. The *Chella* did not survive for long. Just five

months after the incident she was bombed while in port at Marseille. Ablaze but not sinking, she was towed to shallow water and sunk by a French coastal battery.
9. *Orkney Herald*, 10 January 1940, p. 5.
10. Skipper McIntosh was presented to the King and Queen when they made a tour of Scottish ports in March.
11. *Orkney Herald, and Weekly Advertiser and Gazette for the Orkney & Zetland Islands*, 24 January 1940, p.7.
12. Those killed were: Warrant Engineer J.F. Baxter (33); Midshipman J.W. Busk (18); Midshipman R.C. Evans-Lombe (18) and Paymaster Midshipman D.B.P. Pick (19).
13. *Orkney Herald*, 20 March 1940, p. 5.
14. HMS *Norfolk* was quickly repaired on the Clyde and after being fitted with new radar on the Tyne she was back in service again by December 1940. The ship had several connections with the story of Scapa Flow in the early years of the war. Following the sinking of HMS *Royal Oak*, the submarine commanded by Prien had claimed to have sunk HMS *Norfolk*. In fact, the torpedo had missed, exploding in the cruiser's wake.
15. The date that HMS *Afridi* was sunk was the second anniversary of her commissioning into service. Able Seaman Harcus is commemorated on the Portsmouth Naval Memorial.
16. *Orkney Herald*, 17 July 1940, p.6.
17. *Orkney Herald*, 21 August 1940, p.6.
18. For the seven men in the jolly boat (a small clinker-built boat) a terrible ordeal was beginning which would leave only two of them alive. This ordeal lasted some 70 days adrift on the Atlantic before they made landfall in the Caribbean. One of the survivors was killed on his journey back to Britain when his ship was torpedoed. The other survived the war but was haunted by his experiences and committed suicide in 1963. The captain of the *Widder*, Helmuth von Ruckteschell was captured by the Allies and tried for war crimes in 1947. Found guilty, he was sentenced to seven years imprisonment and died in captivity.

19. The squadrons were: No's. 54, 65, 145, 266, and 616.
20. *Orkney Herald*, 30 October 1940, p.6.
21. *Orkney Herald*, 7 November 1940.
22. Lieutenant Colonel 'Jock' Creagh Scott had served with courage during the First World War, winning the DSO, but was a conspiracy theorist and anti-war protestor with extremely strong anti-semitic views.
23. *Orkney Herald*, 30 October 1940, p.6.
24. Seaman Foulis is commemorated on the Tower Hill Memorial, one of at least fifteen Orcadians on that memorial.
25. The MV *Empire Statesman* had begun life as the Genoese registered *Ansaldo VIII* before being renamed the *Ansaldo Ottavo* and then the *Pellice*. On 10 June 1940 she was docked at Newcastle-upon-Tyne and was seized when Italy entered the war. Renamed and requisitioned by the Ministry of War Transport she was handed over to the Newcastle firm of W. Runciman & Co.
26. Another Orcadian Kelday lost his life during the war. Seaman Jerry Wilson Kelday (29) of Kirkwall lost his life when HMS *Curacoa* was struck and split in half by the RMS *Queen Mary* on 2 October 1942. His parents were William and Tomasina Kelday and he left a widow, Maud.
27. Creamola was a soft drink on the form of soluble crystals added to water. It was manufactured in Glasgow until Nestlé stopped production in 1998. It can still be purchased (under the names Krakatoa Foam or Kramola Fizz) from retro sweet shops.
28. *Orkney Herald*, 13 August 1941, p.6.
29. *Orkney Herald*, 27 August 1941, p.5.
30. *Ibid.*
31. *Orkney Herald*, 7 January 1942, p.6.
32. *Orkney Herald*, 7 January 1942, p.6.
33. There are several mysteries surrounding the death of Sgt Matthews. Firstly, the author can find no mention of the crash in the established literature (although there are online accounts), secondly the unit of 3 Group Training Flight is

rather vague while 3 Beam Training Flight was also based at Newmarket at the same time, and thirdly, Sgt Matthews is buried at Yeovil where, presumably, he was from. The crew mix is rather odd with five wireless op / air gunners, three air gunners, the pilot and a flight engineer. Two of the crew survived, although they were injured.

34. F / Sgt Velzian is buried in Bucharest along with those of his crew who perished.
35. John Campbell is commemorated on the Tower Hill Memorial.
36. Sergeant Goodsir is buried at Annan Cemetery.
37. All of the crew were subsequently buried at Lorient Communal Cemetery. They were: Sgt A.F. Galley (pilot); Sgt K.J. Alexander (observer); Sgt W.G. Roddy, RCAF (air observer); Sgt J.D.R. Heddle (wireless op / air gunner) and F / Sgt G.C. Barrie (air gunner).
38. Sergeant Matthieson is buried at Coningsby Cemetery. The crew were: P / O W.B. Carlyle, RCAF (pilot); P / O G.R. Hanna, RCAF (observer); Sgt A.M. Blyth (wireless operator / air gunner); Sgt J.K. Marshman, RAAF (unknown); Sgt R.M. Mathieson (air gunner); F / Sgt A.G. Gibson, RCAF (air gunner); F / Sgt J.E.S. Walker, RCAF (air gunner); Sgt J. Teevin (wireless op / air gunner); LAC H.R. Forster (ground crew) and AC1 G.E. Smith (ground crew).
39. Squadron Leader Harrold now lies in the Khartoum War Cemetery in Sudan. His headstone bears the inscription: 'Treasured Memories of our dear Jock, Loving, Gentle, Ever Kind'.
40. The crew who were killed were: Sgt M.H. Riddell (pilot); Sgt L. Sutherland (2nd pilot); P / O E. Whitaker (observer); Sgt G.P. Taylor (wireless op / air gunner); F / Sgt C.W. Buchner, RCAF (air gunner). The survivor, Sgt Rodney Webber, RCAF was later repatriated and posted to 158 Squadron. He was killed, as a Warrant Officer, on an operation to Essen on the night of 3 April 1943.
41. *Orkney Herald, and Weekly Advertiser and Gazette for the Orkney and Zetland Islands*, 5 February 1941, p.6.

42. *Ibid.*
43. *Orkney Herald*, 14 April 1943, p.4.
44. *Orkney Herald*, 14 April 1943, p.3.
45. *Orkney Herald*, 16 June 1943, p.7.
46. AVM Collishaw's participation in the Wings for Victory campaign would prove to be amongst his last duties in the RAF as he was retired on medical grounds shortly afterwards and spent the rest of the war as a Civil Defence Regional Air Liaison Officer.
47. *Orkney Herald*, 23 June 1943, p.5.
48. The crew were: F / Lt G.U. Pulford (pilot); Sgt D.M. Hughes (flight engineer); Sgt J.W. Barnden (navigator); Sgt W.F.W. Jones (bomb-aimer); Sgt R.E.T. Burns (wireless op / air gunner); Sgt W. Skea (mid-upper air gunner); Sgt J.P. Van Der Linde (rear air gunner).
49. The author would be interested in any information which might be furnished on this intriguing story.
50. *Orkney Herald, and Weekly Advertiser and Gazette for the Orkney & Zetland Islands*, 15 May 1945, p.6.

Index

Agricultural and farming, 19–20, 95, 114–15
Air raids, 22–31, 51, 77
    Clydeside blitz, 55
Air Raid Precautions (ARP), 25–6, 52, 95–101, 109
    blackout, 21
        see also Crime
        fatal accident as a result of, 53
    first aid training, 40
    lack of firefighting equipment, 97
Air Training Corps, 65
Arctic convoys, 112–14
    see also Royal Navy and Merchant Navy
Army, 20, 86
    Linklater, Major Eric, 80
    units,
        2/20th Australian Infantry,
        Day, Pvt David Rendall, 126
        Royal Artillery,
        McDonald, Gnr William M., 128
        Partner, Gnr George, 126
        Rosie, Pvt Thomas, 15
        Tucker, Pvt Thomas, 125

Battle of Britain, 38
Birsay, ix, 8
Burray, 3, 15, 42, 80

Charities, 58–9
    Balfour Hospital, 59
    Charitable fund of Naval officer-in-charge, Kirkwall, 59
    comforts fund, 37
    drunkenness, 42
    Finland Fund, 22
    Fighter fund, 47–9
        see also Charities, Spitfire fund
    Kirkwall & District Nursing Association, 59
    Red Cross, 12, 37–8
    RNLI, 59
    RNLI Shipwrecked Mariners' Society, 30, 59
    Royal Naval Benevolent Trust, 59
    Royal Naval & Marine Orphan Home, 59

Salute the Soldier Week, 119–20
salvage campaigns, aluminium, 38
Scottish Clan Evacuation Plan, 55–6
Spitfire fund, 40–1
Toc-H club, 8, 43–4, 59
Warships Week, 77–9, 82–91, 110
War Weapons Week, 55–8, 59–71, 84, 110
Wings for Victory Week, 79–80, 101–102, 106–12
Christmas and Hogmanay, 11–15, 35, 50–1, 73, 76
Conscientious objectors, 20–1
Crime, 105
  black-market offences, 71–2, 120–2
  blackout related offences, 21–2, 105
  curfew offences, 36
  motoring offences, 76
  poaching, 18–19
  theft, 19, 45–6

D-Day, 119

Ebay, 18
Entertainment, 29–30, 103–104, 118
  see also Sport
  cinema, 43–4, 101–103
  ENSA, 13, 88

Kirkwall Amateur Dramatics Society, 58, 88

Fair Isle, 77
Fishing, 116
  vessels,
    Colleague, 11
    Compagnus, 11
    Swanney, Deckhand James, 11
  vulnerability to aerial attack, 10–11

Home Guard, 53, 62, 64–5, 85–6, 87, 95–7, 102–103, 109
Horne, Drum Major David, 119

Italian PoW's, 80–2, 125
  see also Lamb Holm

Kirkwall, viii, 3, 6, 11, 13–15, 18, 23, 31, 36, 40–1, 46, 52, 87, 99–101, 103, 110, 119–20, 126–7
  Allan, PC David H., 6–8

Lamb Holm, 80
  Italian Chapel, 80–2

Mainland, viii
Merchant Navy, 20, 116
  Anglo-Saxon, SS
    Duncan, Second Officer Alistair St Clair, 42–3

Cape Corso, SS, 82–3
   Campbell, 2nd Radio Officer John Alexander Paris, 82
Diplomat, SS, 50–1
   Foulis, Seaman John Kent, 50–1
Empire Statesman, MV,
   Henderson, Seaman Magnus Leith, 51
Orkney Direct Line, 17–18, 30
   Rota, AS, 17–18
   Tulloch, A/S James, 18
Morale, 101, 103

Neven-Spence, B.H.H., MP, 116–17
North Ronaldsay, 126

Papa of Westwray, viii

Rationing, controls and shortages, 15–19, 39–42, 44–5, 54–5, 76, 97, 101, 114, 117–18, 120
   Dig for Victory, 117–19
   poor food supplies to Stromness, 97, 99–100
   Vegetables for Victory, 104–105
Recipes,
   lighthouse pudding, 55
   wartime lemon curd, 54

Religion, 103–104
   lack of piety, accusations by Rev. David Bell, 73–5
   St Magnus canteen, 75
Royal Air Force, 20, 90
   Bomber Command, 91–3, 102, 105–106, 122–3
   Coastal Command, 102
   Harrold, Squadron Leader Johnoneyman Clouston, 52, 93
   RAF Grimsetter (RAF Kirkwall), 40
   RAF Skaebrae, 34, 46–7
   units,
      3 Group Training Flight, Matthews, Sgt Albert David, 77
      15 Operational Training Unit, Sutherland, Sgt Leonard, 93–4
      55 Operational Training Unit, Goodsir, Sgt Jacques Thorfin, 91–2
      106 Squadron, Mathieson, Sgt Robert Muir, 93
      156 Squadron, Heddle, Sgt John David Robert, 92
      166 Squadron, Skea, Sgt William, 123

INDEX

178 Squadron,
    Velzian, F/Sgt James Robert, 81
255 Squadron,
    Kelly, F/Sgt Robert Dickson, 116
WAAF,
    Mason, Corporal Georgina Harcus, 124
Royal Navy, 20, 43, 86
    Afridi, HMS, 31–2
        Harcus, A/S/ Gillies, 31–2
    Ark Royal, HMS, 1
    Courageous, HMS, 1–3
        Delday, Stoker 1st Class John Liddle, 1–3
        Robertson, Stoker 1st Class George, 3
    Curacoa, HMS, 8
    Daisy II, HMD, 4
        Gatt, Skipper John, 4
    Fleet Air Arm, 34, 86
        804 Squadron, 51
        Robin, HMS, 40
    Grenade, HMS, 31
    Griffin, HMS, 32
    Hampshire, HMS, xi
    Home Fleet, xi, 101, 120
    Hood, HMS, 29
    Imperial, HMS, 31–2
    Iron Duke, HMS, 6–7
    Kingston Cornelian, HMT, 15
        Bruce, Seaman Norman Duncan, 15

Narborough, HMS, xi
Ness, HMS, 83
Norfolk, HMS, 5, 22, 29
Opal, HMS, xi
Pegasus, HMS, 3, 5–7
Renown, HMS, 29
Repulse, HMS, 29
Royal Oak, HMS, 3–10, 32, 125–6
    Baker, Boy 1st Class William Gemmell Mitchell, 8
    Johnston, Stoker Herbert, 5, 7–8
    Moar, Stoker 2nd Class James William, 8
Royal Naval Reserve (RNR), 3, 15
Sutherland, Seaman John R., 3

Orkney barriers, 32–3, 80, 120, 125–6
Orphir, 31

Protected area status, 9, 99–100
    curfew, 34–5, 50

Scapa Flow, xi, 26, 30–1
    aerial defences, 33–5, 46–7, 51
    visitor centre, xii
Scottish Airways, 30
Shapinsay, 123
Skara Brae, viii, ix

South Ronaldsay, 93
Sport,
    boxing, 118–19
    football, 14, 90–1
        Kirkwall City, 14
        Kirkwall Rovers, 14
        Scottish Command XI, 91
        Stromness Athletic, 14
    table-tennis, 90
St Ola, 41, 77
Stromness, 8, 18, 31, 48–9, 52, 92, 94, 107, 116, 127

Stronsay, 46

Twatt, 3

VE Day, 124–6
VJ Day, 126–8

Westray, 11–12, 50
Women's Rural Institute, 53–4, 83–4
Women's Voluntary Society (WVS), 12, 37–8, 41–2